FROM WHENCE COMETH MY HELP

FROM WHENCE COMETH MY HELP

The African American Community at Hollins College

Ethel Morgan Smith

University of Missouri Press ❖ Columbia and London

Copyright © 2000 by
The Curators of the University of Missouri
University of Missouri Press, Columbia, Missouri 65201
Printed and bound in the United States of America
All rights reserved
5 4 3 2 1   04 03 02 01 00

Library of Congress Cataloging-in-Publication Data

Smith, Ethel Morgan, 1952–
    From whence cometh my help : the African American community
at Hollins College / Ethel Morgan Smith.
        p. cm.
    Includes bibliographical references (p.) and index.
    ISBN 0-8262-1260-3 (alk. paper)
        1. Afro-Americans—Virginia—Hollins—History. 2. Afro-
    Americans—Virginia—Hollins—Biography. 3. Hollins (Va.)—
    History. 4. Hollins (Va.)—Race relations. 5. Hollins College—
    Biography. 6. Hollins College—History. I. Title.

F234.H65 S55 1999
975.5'792—dc21   99-047290

♾™ This paper meets the requirements of the
American National Standard for Permanence of Paper
for Printed Library Materials, Z39.48, 1984.

Jacket design: Stephanie Foley
Text design and composition: Vickie Kersey DuBois
Printer and binder: Thomson-Shore, Inc.
Typefaces: Carlton, Florentine, Korinna, Goudy, VAG Rounded

Frontispiece: Women with baskets of laundry, *The Spinster*, 1903, p. 31.

For Mrs. Mary Emma Bruce
and the Silent Voices of the Hollins Community,
both past and present

I will lift up mine eyes unto the hills,
    from whence cometh my help.
My help cometh from the LORD,
    which made heaven and earth.

—*Psalm 121*

Levavi Oculos ("I have lifted my eyes") is the motto for Hollins College.

Contents

Prologue

This book brings to an end an experience that enriched and changed my life. I began this project as a graduate student in the creative writing program at Hollins College, in Roanoke, Virginia. But the journey actually started more than a century before I was born. According to the Census Bureau Report in Roanoke, Virginia, Charles Lewis Cocke, a white slaveholder, arrived in Roanoke County to establish Hollins College in 1842. In addition to his wife, Susana, and their children, he brought with him sixteen enslaved people. The report also shows that a twenty-eight-year-old "mulatto" man by the name of George Newman arrived with them and lived in the Cocke household. In 1860, 10 percent of the African American population were "mulattos," and one third of the population of Roanoke County was enslaved—2,640 individuals. The number of slaves had increased from 1840, when 1,553 were enslaved, to 1850, when 2,510 were enslaved. Contributing to this increase were the earliest students of Hollins, who came to the area with enslaved people as well.

After the Civil War, the term *servants* was applied to the enslaved people. They lived in a community called "Oldfield," a name derived from references to "that old field," the ruined farmland where the slaves or servants lived. In an effort to rid themselves of the language of slavery, the descendants of the original "Oldfield" now identify themselves and the area in which they live as the Hollins Community.

Since I had not been a formal student in sixteen years, I was determined to make my experience in graduate school meaningful. An opportunity to add significance to my graduate program presented itself when I inquired about "rumors"—the term my professors used—regarding Hollins College and slavery. I spent time with the dining-hall workers, all of whom are black, and discovered that most of them lived in a small community adjoining the college. They invited me to worship with them in their church.

In the past, history was generally concerned with studies and analyses of groups, giving little credence, however, to the narratives of individuals in those groups. Thus, African American history has in large part been appropriated by whites and told from an outsider's view. The point of view of African Americans has in many instances remained silent—not because there was nothing to say, but because these voices lacked a medium with which to claim their history.

I believe the history of the Hollins Community is the history of every American—struggling with who we are, where we came from, and how we see ourselves in the world. One of the most significant steps to self-respect involves the unearthing of documents, the giving of voices to those who have been silent, the claiming of images. Communities no less than individuals need to know their origins and heritage in order to break the silence of their history and claim the past. By helping the Hollins Community to see its past and continuing role in the shaping of American history, *From Whence Cometh My Help* is an important step in furthering the esteem in which a valuable but dying community is held.

The surviving stories from the Hollins Community offer a living study of what happened to African Americans in a specific part of the rural South as people shifted, generation by generation, from bondage, to economic servitude, to constrained independence. The community remains intact. Its church and cemetery and confines live on. Not much has changed, except for the addition of a waterline, which the local government finally extended to the area's houses in 1989. But as the eldest inhabitants die off, with them go the stories of the many who came before them. This book is an attempt to hear some of the silent voices of the Hollins Community.

Acknowledgments

I wish to thank Mrs. Mary Emma Bruce for graciously sharing details of her life with me. Her generosity not only enriched my knowledge of the Hollins Community, but she offered me an appreciation for everyone who has worked in domestic service, including my own mother, Mrs. Maudie Mae Baker. Without the love and support of Mrs. Bruce, this book would not have been possible. I will forever be indebted to her and her family.

I would also like to express my gratitude to so many others who encouraged and pointed me in the right direction and who willingly read and reread drafts of this manuscript and insisted that I could make it better. Some wrote letters on my behalf, helping to secure grants that gave me the time to work on the book. Others supported me by believing that I could complete this project with the dignity and passion that I felt for it.

I am happy to have the opportunity to thank Gail Adams, Tim Adams, Bonnie Anderson, William Andrews, Alvord Beardsless, Mary Bishop, Kim Connor, Daryl Dance, Richard Dillard, Anna Elfenbein, Bernd Engler, Virginia Fowler, Marianne Gingher, Nikki Giovanni, Cathy Gouge, Patricia Hampl, Beth Harris, Mary Ann Johnson, David Katzman, John Kern, Anna Logan Lawson, Deborah McDowell, Colleen McElroy, Opal Moore, Marilyn Moriarty, Julia Shivers, Harry Smith, Marcus Bernard Smith, Renee Sulipeck, Noelle Sullivan, Leslie Taylor, Cheryl Torsney, Esther Vassar, and Anne Bradford Warner.

I would also like to thank the University of Missouri Press, especially Beverly Jarrett and Julie Schroeder.

I wish to acknowledge the support of the Fulbright Commission, the Hollins Community, Hollins University, Mount Moriah Baptist Church, the National Endowment for the Humanities, the Roanoke Library, the Roanoke Historical Society, the *Roanoke Times and World News*, the Virginia Center for the Creative Arts, the Virginia Foundation for the Humanities and Public Policy, and West Virginia University.

Creating a book is a lengthy process, and there are certainly others who have offered me assistance when I've needed it. If I have left any names from this page, I have done so because of a lack of memory—not a lack of gratitude.

FROM WHENCE COMETH MY HELP

1

In the Beginning

There were bizarre beginnings in old
lands for the making of me.
Margaret Walker

When I first met Mrs. Emma Bruce she was eighty-two years old and holding down three jobs, cleaning houses for three white families. Sundays and
Tuesdays were her only days off. On Tuesdays she visited the sick, shopped,
and cleaned her own house. On Sundays she sang in the choir at Hollins
Community First Baptist Church, which is just around the corner from her
house. Mrs. Bruce is active in many capacitates at her church. "The church has
no debt and a congregation of more than three hundred members," she told me
proudly. The minister is the Reverend Charles Calloway, a big man with a stirring voice from Richmond, Virginia. That church is where I first approached
Mrs. Bruce about talking to me about the history of the community.

I had already spent much time with the workers in the Hollins College dining
hall, asking questions about the historic African American community. They
had invited me to worship with them at their church. I was glad, excited, and
nervous to have the opportunity to meet some of the members of the Hollins
Community. I had only spoken with a few of them who worked in the dining
hall. This would be my first opportunity to visit them in their community.

On a sunny spring Sunday, the first Sunday after Easter, ash trees at the foot
of the Hollins Community had burst in full bloom. Redbud dotted the mountain-
side. A friendly breeze circled the community.

Inside the church, the smell of fried chicken stirred a hunger in me, not just
for food, but for my own growing years, when I attended the New Bethel
Baptist Church in rural Alabama. Everything about the Hollins College First
Baptist felt familiar: The dark-paneled thin walls and the artificial flowers that
graced the tops of the organ and piano. A velvet-looking tapestry of The Last
Supper hung on the wall to the left. Babies cried. Ceiling fans circulated hot
air, even with the air conditioning. Two choirs sang spirituals—"Amazin'
Grace" and "Were You There?" They even sang my favorite: "Lord, Lift Me
Up." I felt at home.

1

I was surprised and delighted when I walked up to Mrs. Bruce, introduced myself, and asked her if she had any interest in meeting with me. She said yes almost before I could complete my sentences. No one else in the community had been willing to talk to me; they had been generally friendly, but guarded. Sometimes at the post office or in the dining hall, I could almost, but not quite, generate a conversation. They were quick to tell me, "I don't know nothing." This made me wonder: What happens to the history of a people not accustomed to writing things down? Does this make oral history fiction? It is usually futile to search for letters, wills, and diaries of the poor and unlettered. Birth and death certificates, tax receipts, and other official records offer us glimpses but do not show everyday life. Because of the paucity of recorded history, Mrs. Mary Emma Bruce is a most precious resource. For her, stories are grounded in the ordinary occurrences of the world between the college and the community.

Our first visit was at her home on Old Mill Drive. We met on Tuesday. "I looked in on the sick this morning. George can do the shopping. And cleaning this house sure can wait," she laughed.

Her grandson, George, lived with her while he attended college at Virginia Tech on a football scholarship. Her granddaughter, Cynthia, lives in Norfolk, Virginia, with her husband, Wendell Thornton, and their two children. Having graduated from Virginia Commonwealth University in Richmond, Cynthia and her husband were expecting their first baby—the first great-grandchild of an overjoyed Mrs. Bruce. At the time of this writing, Cynthia has just completed her Master of Sciences in Education Administration from Old Dominion University, where she is also employed as Acting Associate Director of Admissions.

The Hollins Community is folded between Williamson Road to the south and Carvin's Cove to the northwest. Old Mill is the first street to the right, off of Reservoir Road, which is the main road through the community. From both sides of the road derelict houses and chimneys stand as a reminder of what the area once looked like. The other houses, like Mrs. Bruce's, are ranch-style brick houses with no front porches. These homes had no running water until 1989, when a public improvements project put in a two-hundred-thousand-gallon water storage tank, water and sewer lines, and fire hydrants. The residents had been asking the county for such improvements since at least the early 1970s. Meanwhile, they had survived with turn-of-the-century hard-water wells, recalcitrant septic tanks, and, in many cases, outdoor bathrooms.

It was newsworthy when the Hollins Community finally received running water. In July of 1988, the Roanoke Times and World News *reported that Mrs. Louise Johnson Harris and other citizens of the Hollins Community beamed as an employee for the county utilities department connected a meter to the waterline near the main highway (Reservoir Road). Mrs. Harris told the reporter: "I never thought I'd live to see this day come. You look forward to it, pray and pray for years. . . . It's a dream come true." In September 1989, the newspaper ran another piece on the waterline, with photographs of community members shaking*

Oldfield home at the turn of the century. *The Spinster*, 1903, p. 32.

the hands of government officials who came out to celebrate with the community.
I, myself, couldn't believe that one of the oldest neighborhoods in Roanoke was
just receiving something as basic as running water. I thought of the community as
a tiny third-world nation.

   Mrs. Emma Bruce (she doesn't use Mary), a petite paper-sack brown woman
with sparkling eyes, loved talking to me about the history of Oldfield, the former
name of her community. Black settlements like Oldfield were common to plan-
tations, and some colleges, throughout the South, where there was a need to
house a number of enslaved people and later servants. Other names for such set-
tlements were "the quarter" or "the bottom," but all referred to the usually poor
lands allotted for African American homes. Nowadays, the residents of the
"Oldfield" of Hollins College call their area the Hollins Community, to rid them-
selves of a name that grew out of slavery. The Hollins Community is inhabited
by Mrs. Bruce and others whose ancestors had been enslaved.

   The Hollins Community is described by William Golding in *The Glass Door*
as a "hamlet": "Across the field outside our window is a wood, under Tinker
Mountain. In the wood, and partly visible, is a hamlet, a red church with a
white, clapboard spire. This is a negro village. In the old days, when girls came
to Hollins, they brought their body slaves with them, and sometimes these
slaves stayed on. They settled in the hamlet, and now provide the servants for
the college." [1]

As an older student enrolled in the creative writing program at Hollins College, I worked hard to meet the demands of graduate school, and there were many, both large and small. My business background had made me unaccustomed to talk of "anthologies" and "syllabi." Much of my first semester was spent adjusting to college life once again.

While all of this was happening, my son was also enrolled in college at Wesleyan University in Middletown, Connecticut, which made it necessary for me to find employment. Hollins did not offer a teacher's assistant program. I taught as a substitute teacher in the local high schools and throughout Roanoke County. Substitute teaching served me well in that it offered me valuable experience that I take into the classroom today.

Having to work, of course, ate away at my writing time—the reason I was in graduate school in the first place. But I had no choice but to combine work and school. So when I did write, I devoted myself to it totally.

And then there were my classmates, most of whom were closer to my son's age than mine. I saw them as white, fairly privileged, and with few real responsibilities.

I found myself being pulled toward the Hollins Community, and I began trying to piece together stories whispered around campus about the days of slavery. When I asked my professors in Bradley Hall to tell me about Oldfield, I was told, "Shhhhh . . ." That made me even more curious. I began spending time in the dining hall with the employees, all of whom were black and most of whom lived in the Hollins Community. And if they didn't live there, they once had, or still had family who lived there.

From my research and conversations with the employees, I found that more than 150 years after the founding of the college, 27 of the 124 Hollins Community residents are still employees of the college, performing many of the same tasks as their ancestors had—cooking, cleaning, planting, weeding, mowing—serving the college rather than being served by it.

Situated on thirteen and a half acres of land between the college and Tinker Mountain, the Hollins Community lies on the border of Botetourt and Roanoke Counties, about equally divided between the two. The area is divided into four sections. The first, popularly known to members of the community as Cufftown, named for a Mr. Cuff, the first person to own land in the "Oldfield," marks the entrance to the community; this is also where the elementary school was located. Originally, there were two one-room schools, one in each of the two counties, having one teacher and sixty to seventy pupils in each. Later, the two schools were consolidated into one having seven grade levels: the Hollins Elementary School. The cost of building the school, in 1921, was ten thousand dollars. Each county made a contribution, and the community took on fundraising projects. There is no record of Hollins College contributing any form of financial support. After completing the seventh grade, the students attended Carver High in Salem or Center Academy in Fincastle.

While "it was illegal to educate any black man or woman after 1800, historical notes on Roanoke County and Hollins College suggest that schooling was available for members of the community." Deedie Kagey further speculates that "even though formal school districts were not established until 1846, Oldfield School was known throughout Roanoke County, though its existence is hard to prove." Despite there being no written evidence for such a school, the active role taken by C. L. Cocke, the founder of Hollins College, in the education of slaves is well documented: "He organized and conducted the first school for the slaves in Big Lick (now Roanoke) in 1846, and for twenty years he rode the five miles from Hollins on horseback on Sunday afternoons to instruct them."[2]

Ash Bottom, the second section of the Hollins Community, is located west of the church, near the grove of ash trees. The final two sections are Oldfield (now the underpass, so it exists only in a historical sense) and Rocky Branch, the cut-off to the college that begins directly behind the church and includes the southern portion of the community. Rocky Branch was named for the path where mothers from the community had placed a series of rocks as a guide for their children. This enabled the children to walk to Hollins without having to use the main road, in case they needed their parents while they worked. This information has never been recorded anywhere, but it is rooted in the memory of Mrs. Bruce and other members of the community.

In addition to attending church and spending time with the employees in the dining hall, I also visited the community. On a warm spring Saturday I explored the cemetery of the Hollins Community First Baptist Church, located directly across the street from the church. Because it was spring, the cemetery was overgrown with weeds. Mrs. Bruce told me later that family members hadn't yet held their annual clean-up, which happens in late summer. I was nervous when I first set foot in the cemetery, but once there, I lost myself in the moment. I felt like Alice Walker looking for the grave of Zora Neale Hurston—except I didn't know what I was looking for. But the cemetery told me volumes. The names— Boldens, Bruces, Hunts, Johnsons, Langhornes, Meades, Mortons, Philipots, and Scotts—spoke to me. Of all the places in the world, I knew that the Hollins Community was where I was meant to be. And when I stopped and listened very carefully, I could hear the voices urging me on. I received that experience as a "calling" to move forward with my research. I stopped being so consumed with what I could not find and discovered satisfaction in knowing that all I would find would be valuable.

The names carved on some of the headstones were also the last names of many of the first students to be enrolled at the college. Many of the graves only had rocks placed on them. Families had lived, worked, and died in this community. Sometimes they were young, sometimes old; they were war veterans, mothers, fathers, and children. Absorbing the litany of names and dates I came to appreciate that communities, no less than individuals, need to know their origins—

Example of early housing in Oldfield; note cookware on side of cabin.
The Spinster, 1903, p. 32.

their heritage—in order to gain self-respect. We are as much a product of our communities as we are of our parents.

When I arrived home that Saturday afternoon my telephone was ringing. Reverend Calloway was on the line. He said he heard that I had been seen in the cemetery. He knew who I was—and he told me that I needed permission to go into the cemetery. I apologized and told him I certainly meant no disrespect to the church or the community. I tried to relate to him what I was trying to do— as far as I knew at the time—and how I felt it was not just important, but urgent for me to shed light into the shadows of slavery, to help give voice to those whose lives and achievements were unrecorded and therefore unaccounted for. I asked how to go about getting permission, because I saw my project as offering the community a gift. He said that the members of the church would probably not be interested in talking with me. In all of my life I'd never heard of anyone having to get permission to enter a cemetery. My own life had been so rooted in the black southern Baptist Church.

Hurt and surprised that Reverend Calloway felt this way, I begin to realize what a difficult task I had ahead of me. But I remembered the voices in the cemetery and knew that they wanted me—in fact, were counting on me—to push forward. Reverend Calloway, like many black preachers in the South, is more than just a minister, he is the leader of his community. This realization bothered me as well, because I believe leaders have a responsibility to do right by the people. To me, doing right by the people means addressing issues that directly affect their lives. For instance, when I attended church in the Hollins Community, it was clear to me that there needed to be some discussion about teenage pregnancy, and the responsibilities of both the young men and women. I also believed that there needed to be a college preparation workshop. Mostly women of all ages attended church. If men were present they were usually elderly.

Hollins First Baptist Church, built 1967–1969; Ash Bottom is to the right.
Photo by Opal Moore.

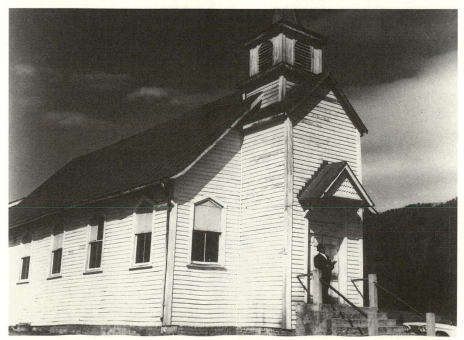

First Baptist Church Hollins; this is the second church, which was replaced in 1969. Photo from Zackery Hunt; in collection of the author.

Cemetery at First Baptist Hollins. Photo by Opal Moore.

Mrs. Bruce had warned me that it may be hard to get folks to talk to me. When I asked why, she replied, "Child, these folks pretend that they are scared of losing their jobs."

"This has nothing to do with their jobs," I said.

"Well, you're probably right since most of them hold down at least two jobs anyway."

"Really?"

"You see, a long time ago, before we had cars, malls, and such, this was a special place to work. Nobody in this community ever went hungry as far as I can remember. And we had our church and later a school. But now, folks can travel to Roanoke and other places to work and live."

"But why wouldn't they be interested in their history?"

"Child, they're not used to anyone being interested in them. They're used to being told what to do only."

It occurred to me how naive I was. I thought they would see me as a benefactor rather than a troublemaker. I looked at Mrs. Bruce and shook my head.

"Don't worry, Child. Some will talk. Our history is all that we have."

Emma Bruce at home, April 1999.
Photo by the author.

Talking to Mrs. Bruce always offers me courage. This time, she explained to me why folks referred to Roanoke as a separate place from the college. For me, Hollins College was located in Roanoke, Virginia, but for members of the Hollins Community it was different; it was the city. For example, in my conversations with community members, a name would be mentioned and I'd ask if the person still lived here. I was then told, "No, he moved away years ago." "Where?" I asked. "Up in Roanoke" was the response. I had to start thinking about the college in a different way—how it was a hundred years ago. Once I changed my mind-set, answers began to come to me in unexpected ways. I understood why I had received so little response from the members of the community: A slave mentality was at work. The language of silence was just as effective as it had been three hundred years ago. No one had raised questions about their relationships and conditions; they just accepted certain practices as tradition.

I thought of other women's colleges in Virginia and researched their early histories. I found that Randolph-Macon Woman's College in Lynchburg wasn't established until 1891 and opened in 1893. Being postbellum and in a more urban setting offered a different ideology. The remoteness of Hollins created a more closed community, making it easier to continue with the tradition of slavery. Randolph-Macon also had a history of generations of African Americans working for them, but that college had educated as many as fifty of the daughters of its domestic and janitorial workers by 1990. Yet at Hollins, only one young woman from the community had ever graduated from the college. The college had not offered the benefits and educational opportunities to its African American employees that it had to its white employees and their families.

Sweet Briar College, just up the road from Randolph-Macon Woman's College, did not open its doors until 1908, making it quite modern. In this case, the African American community that served the college is older than the college itself. I wasn't able to find out how many of the daughters of the workers had attended the college, but I was told by members of the college and its community that many had.

Mary Baldwin College was established in 1842 like Hollins, but unlike Hollins, in 1966, its administration decided that the best way to integrate the college was to enroll the daughters of the workers. An MBC representative I spoke with described it as a "smooth transition." It seemed as though there had been great concern with the living arrangements; thus, the daughters of the workers had all been day students.

This raised the question, why was Hollins College so different from her sister colleges? Why was this college still rooted in antebellum traditions?

I continued my research by visiting the Fishburn Library at Hollins. Deep in the basement was a box marked Servants. I wasn't allowed to borrow the yellowed loose-leaf pages (financial ledgers, for the most part), but I was able to read them uninterrupted, which I did over and over. The librarian apologized for the state of the box, explaining that many important documents had been destroyed or misplaced due to a 1985 flood.

The highlight of that day was when I examined back issues of The Spinster, Hollins College's yearbook. In the 1903 issue I found photographs of some of the earliest members of the community. Lewis Hunt rang the triangle; no one could ring it the way he could. In the photograph, Mr. Hunt wore a carnation on his lapel. Then I stumbled onto a photograph of Caesar Morton. Both men were beaming with pride in their suits, ties, and worn shoes.

But the most stirring photographs were the ones of the women walking with baskets of laundry on their heads. They marched toward the spring, south of the college, to wash the clothes of the students, faculty, and administration. Chills ran over me. Those women could have been from anywhere in the world—Africa, Brazil, the Caribbean, India, or Turkey—but they were from the foothills of the Blue Ridge Mountains, carrying on a tradition that was so old they probably didn't recognize its origins. I felt claustrophobic. I was choking in that hot musty basement of the library; I had to get out for air. I left the books on the table and ran out. I found myself in the Jesse duPont Chapel, three buildings over, where quietness and serenity embraced me. I didn't know why I ran into the chapel, since I had never set foot in it before. As the atmosphere of the chapel soothed me, I realized that for the first time, I had seen members of the community as enslaved people. Intellectually, I had accepted it, but now I had to come to grips with the fact that slavery had existed right here on the grounds upon which I walked, studied, and played tennis.

I returned to the library an hour later and photocopied what information I could. Later at home, I couldn't stop thinking of the people of the community, and I knew that I would never stop thinking about them. The people in those photographs were real to me. I thought of my own mother, who for fifty years labored for a white family, seven days a week, with the exception of the fourth Sunday of every month, when she attended church. As a child, I never understood why my sisters and I couldn't have our mother with us on Christmases and Thanksgivings. I often prayed for Mother to be home with us, even for the weekends. That never happened.

I remember when Mrs. Tomblin, the woman whom Mother worked for, promised Mother her house. Her only living relative lived up North and had no interest in Mrs. Tomblin or the house. Mother repeated this story to us for many years. I dreamed of living in the house with the big screened-in back porch, shady oak trees, and a yard full of flowers. We didn't have flowers because Mother was always too tired. For the first time, I allowed myself to be angry—angry for all of the black women who had and still toiled in the homes and institutions of whites for very little money and no respect. But then I remembered Mrs. Bruce's response when I first asked her how it made her feel that she had worked at the college for more than forty years and still had to work three jobs at age eighty-two: "Child, I thank the Good Lord every day that I have my health and strength."

Unable to find more information, I visited the Roanoke City Library and found more data—and the air conditioner worked. I decided to begin by investigating anything that pertained to the Roanoke area. Looking through every resource having to do with the Roanoke area would prove a daunting task. I explained to the librarian that I didn't know exactly what I was looking for apart from the general nature of my research. She guided me to the library's Virginia Room, which holds personal diaries, Census Bureau reports dating back to 1820, and other archival materials. Some of the diaries had been donated by former students from the college. I spent two weeks going through them hoping to find a photograph or a mention of Oldfield.

The records did not tell me much about the African Americans who were associated with the college in the earliest days. For example, in neglecting to mention the servants of the college, they did not record the fact that generations of blacks have been a major force in the history of the college. Nor did they record the full names of the women who served the college, despite the fact that since it was a women's college, more women than men were employed there (66 percent of the employees were women). That women were so integral to the longevity of the Hollins Community can be seen when one compares the communities of African Americans who lived adjacent to men's colleges such as Davison, Duke, and Hampden-Sydney. Those communities failed to stay intact, since after the Civil War men relocated at a much higher rate than women. Most men who left to find work fully intended to send for their families, but few actually did. Also, many men changed their names after they moved. But women stayed and built communities.

The founding of Hollins College is almost a legend, and ambiguities and contradictions abound. Charles Lewis Cocke, the founder, is thought variously to have owned slaves and to have abhorred slavery. Similarly, the idea that students brought enslaved persons to Hollins College is today often dismissed, although it is true. The fact of settlement by Cocke's and students' slaves is borne out by records as well as the recollections of members of the present-day community. C. L. Cocke is registered in court papers of Roanoke County as the owner of eighteen slaves of his own and four ". . . for Clairborne."[3] Students with the last names of Bolden, Burton, Hunt, Langhorne, and so many others attended the institution before the Civil War. These family names reappear in records of college servants for nearly a hundred years after the founding. This is certainly an instance of enslaved people taking on the names of their enslavers, a very common practice of the time. This also indicates that the first students indeed came to the college with enslaved people, with the label "servants" being applied later.

The labor pool was apparently inadequate to serve the antebellum institution. For filling unskilled positions, Cocke had four options: he could hire white laborers, hire free blacks, use slaves, or purchase additional slaves. The ledgers of the Valley Union Education Society show only one payment to a white laborer, a B. Campbell, who received a total of $86.66 for services in 1857. While 4 percent of Virginia's population in 1840 was free black, few lived in western Virginia and only one is noted in the ledger, Clairborne Scott, who worked for Cocke before moving to Missouri at some point during the Civil War, after having married one of Cocke's female slaves.

> Cocke had arrived in a region where farming wasn't primarily slave-based and local attitudes, largely due to a heavy German presence, were not disposed toward slaveholding. Local farming consisted largely of diversified grain or livestock farms, not plantations, leaving a surplus of [black] agricultural labor. In the Roanoke Valley, the emerging industrial sector easily absorbed the surplus; slaves were hired out extensively by their owners to the Virginia and Tennessee Railroad, the ill-fated Roanoke Valley Railroad, and Big Lick's (Roanoke's former name) new tobacco processing plant.[4]

"And they hired to Charles Lewis Cocke for work at his College," recalled Joseph A. Turner, grandson of Charles Lewis Cocke, in 1926: "They were hired first from their owners and afterwards they hired themselves to Chas . . . Cocke." This practice formed the essential link between the antebellum and postbellum labor pools of the institution. Payment, of course, was to owners of the slaves; slaves were still prevented from bargaining for wages, which is among "the most ordinary decision-making processes of economic life."[5] However, hired men and women slaves became accustomed to working at the institution or for its administrators and faculty.

The benefit of this antebellum practice to Cocke and the Roanoke Valley was a local unskilled labor force that would not experience disruption during the transition to a wage system. There would not be a labor shortage here as in the plantation South, where the wage system would soon break down and thus bring about the use of exploitative means of labor control. Furthermore, freed blacks would always possess their labor as a means for their economic livelihood, unlike their plantation counterparts, who lacked land.

After Emancipation, Hollins Institute (as the college was then known), unlike most of the agricultural South, quickly reestablished a steady supply of labor based on new and continuing residents of the Oldfield settlement. "Within a decade, Hollins came to occupy a monopsony position with respect to [its] labor. While there is no record in the ledgers of payment to any Black worker from 1857 to 1865, most of the female married servants likely remained in the Oldfield community through the Civil War."[6]

Enslaved women tended to remain with their former slaveholders or in the Oldfield settlement after Emancipation, while men sought work elsewhere; assuming that a majority of the original settlers of the community were female slaves held by young women and the founding family, the Cockes, this would in large part account for the persistence of the community. Furthermore, since black exclusion laws in the North precluded settlement in the South, married slaves and slave families seldom left their homes. Elsewhere in the immediate postbellum South, "men opted for more time off, exchanging leisure for money earnings . . . one immediate result of emancipation was a labor 'shortage,' although it was an intentional shortage."[7]

At the very least, no mention whatsoever is made in the minutes of the Valley Union Education Society of any labor difficulties or shortages. If there had been any such problems, they weren't recorded and they aren't remembered. Instead, the college was grievously concerned with currency value and inflation. "In November of 1863, the college set the cost of tuition, room, and board from March to December of 1864 at $800. In March of 1864, 'new currency' was established, and the Board of Trustees stipulated that 'parents must pay enough to buy in the new currency the amount of the first payment due March 16, 1864. In August, tuition, room, and board for one-half of the usual fee period was set at nearly $750—in nominal terms, nearly twice the previous year's fees.' "[8]

Cocke's central role as educator and benefactor created unique conditions at Hollins Institute that helped to solidify the roles of blacks and whites and instill a mutual loyalty among the two races. By contrast, the rebellion of plantation slaves throughout the South was not only against economic disenfranchisement, but also against the continuance of paternalistic relations between themselves and their former owners. "Since many of those hired by the founders as slaves came to work for Cocke as free people, his roles as the supervisor of their labors and their general benefactor were strengthened and perpetuated, and the college's authoritative role in the life of its labor force was firmly established. Once employed as free workers at the college, where they were invariably dubbed 'servants,' male workers were supervised by Cocke and females by Susanna Pleasants Cocke, his wife." As Frances Niederer writes, " 'Miss Susanna' took care of the domestic matters," and "Charles Lewis did everything else."[9]

The net effect of this model was mutual loyalty on the part of the college and its employees, based on paternalistic relationships and simple hierarchy; this promoted flexibility in wage payments, labor relations, and methods of affecting internal structural changes. At the same time, the college enjoyed the stability of an internalized labor market usually only available to large firms with a high degree of bureaucratic control in their operations. This odd congruence, plus the recalcitrant development of other economic opportunities for the Oldfield community residents, "ensured that the unique relationship of the college and community would continue despite pressure to modernize and cut costs and despite the economic advancement of blacks in other parts of the country. The College set about paying employees regularly in 1867."[10]

What would in ten years resemble a regular system of payments began as sporadic allotment of provisions, cash, and other compensation. The board department store functioned as a general store for servants: wages were paid in everything from shoes to bacon to bricks. This measure was, of course, a convenience in difficult economic times and ensured that "servants" would not go hungry, although there was little chance of that, since many in the community spent their workdays preparing and serving food. According to Mrs. Bruce, the workers were allowed to take the food that was left over at the end of the day. But perhaps times were tighter in the earlier days of the college, necessitating payment in foodstuffs. Besides cash and provisions, other forms of compensation included the payment of servants' accounts, merchandise orders, and medical care, which were provided by the institution.

The complete irregularity of payment dates indicates that cash payments in kind were at servants' requests. Also, while servants had assumed the freedom of bargaining for their wages, their employer still made other economic transactions on their behalf. "The College was an intermediary where the alternatives were poor at best: Freedmen's bank [originally set up to aid destitute blacks] had collapsed by 1870, leaving Blacks throughout the South at the mercy of the country storekeeper-cum-banker, who often left rural Blacks in 'debt peonage.' "[11]

Wages and percentages of compensation in cash, provisions, and other compensation are summarized in Table 1 and reflect the same divisions that appear on the college ledgers (1861–1867, 1867–1871, and 1872–1873). The disparity in payments to male and female servants is less evident in monetary terms than in the percentages in which each gender chose to be paid in cash. In the period from 1867 to 1871, the women obtained almost 70 percent of their payment in cash, greatly contrasting with the men, who received only about 30 percent in cash. Female servants were either more reluctant to ask one of the male Cockes for compensation other than cash, or else they relegated this duty to males in the family and community. Except for their dealings with Susanna Cocke, the women were apparently less familiar with the administration than were the men.

Table 1 Payments to Servants, 1861–1873

Ledger of 1861–1867

Male Servants

Number Employed: 8		
Monthly wage (approx.)	$7.50	
Payment in cash	$381.32	52.6%
Payment in provisions	74.21	10.2%
Other compensation	269.22	37.3%
Gross compensation	724.75	100.0%

Female Servants

Number Employed: 3		
Monthly wage (approx.)	$4.27	
Payment in cash	$122.50	79.7%
Payment in provisions	4.66	3.0%
Other compensation	26.50	17.3%
Gross compensation	153.66	100.0%

Ledger of 1867–1871

Male Servants

Number Employed: 12		
Monthly wage	$10.00–14.00	
Payment in cash	$872.31	30.9%
Payment in provisions	581.66	20.6%
Other compensation	1,366.45	48.5%
Gross compensation	2,820.42	100.0%

Female Servants

Number Employed: 23		
Monthly wage		
—Washerwomen	$10.00	
—Chambermaids	6.00–7.00	
Payment in cash	$860.27	69.0%
Payment in provisions	116.46	9.4%
Other compensation	268.49	21.6%
Gross compensation	1,245.22	100.0%

Ledger of 1871–1873

Male Servants
Number Employed: 9
Monthly wage $10.00–12.00

Payment in cash	$314.54	66.2%
Payment in provisions	92.80	19.5%
Other compensation	68.13	14.3%
Gross compensation	475.47	100.0%

Female Servants
Number Employed: 18
Monthly wage
—Washerwomen $10.00–12.00
—Chambermaids 6.00

Payment in cash	$584.09	65.5%
Payment in provisions	77.20	8.7%
Other compensation	230.05	25.8%
Gross compensation	891.34	100.0%

Source: Business notes in Hollins College Special Collections.

The degree of job definition further distinguished male and female servants from each other. Women servants bore the double burden of gender and race. Their obligations as laborers outside the home made both their domestic and work roles unlike those of most southern white females. At the same time, their central role within their own family life in most cases left them with more extensive family duties. Unlike eighteenth- and nineteenth-century white fathers and husbands, enslaved black men exerted no legal control over their families. Although in one respect this arrangement freed enslaved women from the oppression of patriarchal marriage, they were instead directly subjected to the power of all of the men, a less constrained and thus ultimately more devastating form of domination.

The black women who worked at Hollins College as slaves and later as servants were defined by the tasks they performed, unfairly sentencing them to anonymity in terms of written history. But why were there only three women listed as paid employees in the 1861–1867 ledger, and twenty-three in the next ledger? From my research, I learned that after the Civil War, women tended not to leave home as rapidly as men did, making it probable that some of the enslaved women, after Emancipation, gradually assimilated into college employment as servants after 1867. Chances were, the twenty-three women listed as employees after the war had already performed those same tasks—as slaves—before.

As salaries were regularized in 1872, the high end of men's average wages fell slightly to a maximum of twelve dollars per month, while the pay range for washerwomen rose, so that men's and washerwomen's scales matched at ten to twelve dollars monthly. The earning gap between men and women essentially closed: the eighteen women servants made up 66 percent of the workforce, which they had in the period before, but they earned 65 percent of total wages paid instead of the approximately 31 percent in the period from 1867 to 1871. By 1872 specified monthly salaries nearly always appeared in ledger margins, and workers were employed consistently through the session, from September to July. The workforce and the sorts of positions to be filled by unskilled workers—washerwomen, chambermaids, or male laborers—were firmly defined, and wage payments were regularized and dependable.

Despite the intimate role they played in sustaining the life of the college, the humanity of the African American workers was more than ignored; in fact, students were discouraged from any attempt to acknowledge their "servants" as people. In the college catalog of 1876, the rule of William Johnston, associate principal, was reprinted for the first time since 1836: "No familiarity with servants is allowed. Any failure on the part of servants to discharge their duties, not noticed by the officers, should be promptly reported to the Associate Principal."[12] The unskilled labor force of Hollins Institute was thus set apart and defined by a system that would stay in place until the 1940s. This dehumanizing, paternalistic system takes on symbolic proportions when one considers the fact that Hollins College, a women's college, was served largely by women, most of whose names remain unknown.[13]

Meet Julius Caesar of Hollins College
The Most Widely Known Colored Man in Virginia

> Our ancestors are an ever widening
> circle of hope.
>
> Toni Morrison

Six weeks had passed since I had interviewed Mrs. Bruce. I felt frustrated, and I was behind on my classwork. Money was tight. It was the beginning of the short term at the college, the period between Christmas and the second semester. I had one more semester to complete my graduate work.

Worried about money, I telephoned the financial aid officer at my son's university and made arrangements for his return. She knew that I had always lived up to my obligations and we quickly agreed on terms. I applied for a "parent plus" loan of two thousand dollars, which enabled me to manage financially until my income tax refund arrived. So I could put off worrying about money. This was a most exhausting time in my life; my creative energy and spirit were zapped. I tried to remain focused on my Hollins Community research—I didn't want to lose sight of the bigger picture because of the technicality of not having financial resources.

My nerves were on edge because my graduate program was nearing an end, and I needed employment, which possibly meant moving away from Roanoke. I wasn't ready to leave Mrs. Bruce or the Hollins Community. There was so much more work to be done. The first steps I took in finding a job were revising my vita and applying for teaching positions at colleges and universities in the immediate area. After I worked on getting a position, I caught up on my thesis work.

I didn't know where to look for more information. After Reverend Calloway's warning about the cemetery, I felt awkward about attending church. But I couldn't stop thinking about the Hollins Community. And no matter how many times I said out loud, "early students came to college with enslaved people," I found it to be unbelievable. And probably always would.

When I first arrived at the college as a graduate student in 1989, a feeling of surrealism was as much of a presence as my book bag. I accepted it as part of being back in college after sixteen years. The place felt familiar with its beautiful Georgian-styled buildings and perfect grounds. I imagined Hollins as it must have been a hundred years earlier: My first observation was the noise, not from

19

the activities of students and faculty members, but by workers. Something was always being clipped, chopped, cut, mowed, painted, planted, raked, scraped, seeded, washed, or weeded. But perhaps a hundred years ago, before the invention of so much machinery, there was less noise. Then it occurred to me why the college was so familiar: it was a plantation. For two days I spent a good portion of time sitting on the front porch of East Building, where there must be more than a dozen green rocking chairs: I wanted to rock myself back to slavery. I saw the women from the community carrying baskets of laundry on their heads to the spring south of the college. I heard them talking. I felt their presence. They were pleased that I was there. I wanted to know so much about them. Their favorite color? Food? Their hopes and dreams? What they thought about the young women at the college? What happened to their birth families, whom they had left to come to Hollins? How they must have missed them. But that's what slavery was about—leaving loved ones behind.

I called Mrs. Bruce for another interview.

She was feeling a "little prickly" during this second interview. This time I looked around her house and wasn't as nervous as I had been before. Her house comforted me. It reminded me of my own grandmother's house. Her prizewinning African violets and other flowers bloomed on every table and windowsill. As a gardener myself, I asked for her advice on growing plants. She gave it proudly and generously, as she did everything.

Photographs of her family covered her walls, along with clocks and pictures of the traditional-looking Jesus. She was most proud of an old, oval-framed, black-and-white photograph of a proud couple dressed in their best clothes: her grandparents. I asked her if she remembers them.

"I can never forget them. They're always with me."

"Did they work at Hollins?"

"We all did. It was a good job, Miss Smith. We always had food, a place to live, and even our own church after a while. And before we had our own church, the community was invited to worship with the Enon Baptist Church. We knowed a lot of folks a lot worst off."

"Mrs. Bruce, you cannot call me Miss Smith. My name is Ethel." She laughed, and I asked, "what is your relationship to the college now?"

"I'm retired."

"Other than not working, what does that mean? Do you receive any benefits?"

"None."

"How long did you work there?"

"Forty-six years."

"How does it make you feel that you worked for forty-six years and have no retirement benefits?"

"Well, I see it this way: The Good Lord sees fit to give me my health and strength so that I can work and take care of myself. What can I be but thankful?"

"Other than a retirement plan, what else would you like to have received from the college?"

"Education. Education. That's what the college is all about. All of the years that our people put in should have earned us an education. And to this day only one child from this community has ever graduated from the college."

"Who was she?"

"Pam. Pamela Meade."

"Why do you think she's the only one?"

"Well, she come from two of the oldest families in the community, the Morton and Meades. It was a big to-do about it. There was even a write-up in all the newspapers about her."

Caesar Morton. Hollins Archives.

I found the following article in the "Servants" box in the Hollins library basement. No author's name was attached.

The Legacy of Caesar Morton

More than 100 years of family travail and dedication will have preceded her when Pamela Denise Meade mounts the stage on Front Quad to receive her diploma this May. Pamela, a descendant of two of the oldest families connected with Hollins—the Mortons and the Meades—will become the first of Caesar Morton's great grandchildren to graduate from the college he loved and diligently served.

Caesar Morton probably was born a slave in the 1850's to Nathan Morton of Appomattox County, Virginia. Nathan's wife is uncertain, but Sarah Morton, frequently listed near Nathan in college records, may have been she. The ledger of Hollins Institute first mentions Nathan in December 1866, when he earned ten dollars. Later ledgers record the employment of Nathan and his brothers George and Caesar, the latter having given his name to Nathan's son.

Although Caesar Morton the younger himself said he had worked at Hollins "ever since the first year Lee surrendered," college records do not name him until 1869. In that year he was paid nineteen dollars for five months of work. Tradition holds that this work was to pump air for the reed organ that Hollins acquired after the Civil War. Evidently he was still a child, for later his small account was combined with his father's and only reappeared separately in 1873.

There is no evidence that Caesar received any formal education. Nevertheless, all accounts agree that he was one of the wittiest and cleverest people ever at Hollins. Once, having attended a large and pretentious wedding, he was asked if he had had anything good to eat. "No, sir," he said. "They didn't give you nothing but a little lemonade and cake. Folks thats ris in the world don't give you nothing. It's folks thats trying to rise that strains themselves." On another occasion, asked by a librarian to recommend a book, he replied, "Send her *Pilgrim's Progress*. I don't hear much about that book these days." Over the years Caesar picked up some French and, when waiting tables in the dining room, he delighted in confusing students with: "Miss, shav *lait* or *l'eau* or *lactum?*" (Miss, will you have milk or water or buttermilk?)

Caesar Morton died in 1929, having served the college chiefly as head waiter for well over half a century. A long eulogy appeared in *The Hollins Alumnae Quarterly*, but perhaps more fitting to the man was the epithet given him by the students in 1922: *Vir Sapientissimus*.

Of one of Caesar Morton's near contemporaries, Henry Meade, a plasterer and cement finisher, much less is known. Henry was a skilled laborer who helped to erect West Building in 1900. He too worked for many years at Hollins, and he is remembered by one source as "a great big good-looking man." He and his wife, Mary Bice, had a son George who married one of Caesar and Betty Morton's daughters, Grace Ellen.

These two, George Meade, who worked for the college, and Grace Morton, were Pamela Meade's grandparents. Their son George, Pamela's father, recently retired from Hollins after 43 years in the dining room and Little Theater. His wife Alease Meade currently is employed in the mail room.When Pamela steps up to receive her diploma and shakes hands from President Brownlee, four generations of Mortons and Meades will be behind her. The graduation of every Hollins senior is a splendid event, but Pamela's is extra splendid because her family has given so much to make Hollins College what it is. We honor her, we honor her family.[1]

"Did you attend Pam's graduation?" I asked Mrs. Bruce.

"Child, we wouldn't have missed such an event. Was better than the big weddings the white folks used to have." Mrs. Bruce laughed.

"Why do you think that Pam Meade was the only person in the community to graduate from the college?"

"It was the time."

"What do you mean?"

"Everyone, or so it seemed, wanted to enroll one and only one black in the late sixties and seventies. Since the college hadn't done so, it was a good opportunity. And they played up the fact that her relatives had been such a part of the college. Plus, of all the folks in the community, Caesar and Nathan Morton were the first to own land."

In 1868, for $250, "cash in hand paid," Caesar Morton obtained about twenty-five acres from a Samuel and Elizabeth Ronk. This was a considerable sum, just under a year's manufacturing wage in Botetourt County, Virginia. It is not known where he received such a sum at age fifteen. A year later, his brother Nathan paid $118 to the estate of a Mildred Goodman for a thirteen-acre parcel. He purchased another five acres from this estate four years later for $150, and another tract for $300 in 1880.[2]

"Do you know of others in the community who owned land early on?"

"Two more families became landowners after the railroad came. Mary Meade purchased a five-acre plot." It was located on the waters of Carvin's Creek, near Hollins Institute; she paid forty dollars for it in 1896. Four years later, Malinda Bolden spent ten dollars for 130 poles of W. G. Nininger's land. Thereafter, lands in the community were transferred amongst the resident families. In 1907 Caesar and Betty Morton, along with three other family members, granted outright 6 acres and 100 poles adjoining the Cocke family's land to Richard Morton.[3]

"That should have made them pretty financially well-off."

"Well, that would be true if they had held onto the land."

"What do you mean?"

"Well, when times got tight, many of the folks sold their land back to white folks in secret."

"Do you think Mr. Morton sold his land?"

"I don't know, but Caesar was smart from what I know. When he died he was written about in newspapers everywhere."

Meet Julius Caesar, of Hollins College; In Service 67 Years
February 18, 1927

Forty Years as Head Waiter; Now He's Retired—Speaks French, Has Beaucoup Repartee—Humorist, Too.

> "Imperial Caesar turned to clay."
> "Will stop a hole to keep the dust away."
> "Say them words again Mr. Staples: I want to shoot 'em at Mr. Joe Turner."

That, in brief, is Julius Caesar, who has been in the service of Hollins College for sixty-seven years, forty of which he spent as head waiter of the institution.

Today Caesar is an old man in years but not in spirit, for he has the exuberance of eternal youth. Upon seeing him for the first time one is reminded of the vanishing type of Southern colored gentlemen immortalized in Southern literature as Uncle Remus and kindred characters; and of the plantations and cotton fields and bedtime stories for children.

Caesar refuses to be bowed down by the weight of years. He stands with head tilted backward in spite of the slight stoop in body, and relates in an inimical manner a few of his experiences at Hollins.

One watches him with an interest. He is smiling, bubbling over with the kind of humor that is peculiarly characteristic of the Southern colored man of the sixties, and one sees a panorama of the days that he has outlived.

He's Bald.

The top of his head is bald but there is a rim of gray hair and a gray mustache which is thinning. Most of his teeth are gone but he manages to chew tobacco effectively and what few wrinkles there are on his face appear to be caused by a natural smile rather than by the ravages of old age.

His conversational abilities are enhanced by emphatic gesticulation—not carried to the extreme, but used in proportion to the urging of an innate jovial disposition. For this reason one listens to Caesar instead of talking so much to him.

Caesar Morton—for that is his real name—is perhaps more widely known than any other colored man in Virginia. Thousands of students have come and gone during the time he has been at Hollins. The records say that he first came to the college as a boy in his 'teens. With the exception of a few months he has worked there continuously ever since as cart boy and waiter. In recent years he retired from the dining room and was given the position of messenger in the business office. In 1925 he was retired entirely on a small pension.

How Old Is He?

"How old am I?" he parries to a question. "Don't know exactly, but I know it was just after the surrender when I come to Hollins."

Caesar is careful with his English but more so with his French. That language is his specialty. In fact, nothing gives him greater pleasure than to discover he is a better linguist than the one to whom he is talking.

Fortunately, we had been warned about this and endeavored not to fall into the error of saying Frenchy things to Caesar, not even to tell him that we preferred l'eau to lait, or lactium with our dinner.

A "good morning Caesar," is met with a clearly enunciated "Bon jour, Monsieur," and when he tells you that his health is good he follows up with the question "Comment allez-vous?"

"I like to show 'em I've been to school some myself," he explained.

"But tell us something about Hollins—what did they have here in the early days Caesar?"—the question being asked with the thought that it would be too bad to let him discover how meager our French vocabulary really was.

Caesar's Educated.

"Just the main building," he replied, indicating the structure. "That used to be called the St. John's building, had a fireplace in every room. I carried wood for them every day; didn't have any steam heat then."

A look of reminiscence came into his eyes. "When I first come here there wont know Hollins College like you see now; just one building with boards still over the windows. If they had fifteen students it was called a good year." He laughed.

"I used to catch rain water for the girls to wash their hair, and took it to 'em every day—didn't like the hard water—but it was funny when mail time come—we drove a wagon to Salem and to Bonsack and to Big Lick to get the mail and meet the guests." At this point Caesar could not suppress his humor. He reached over to tap the arm of the listener and said: "But the guest and mail didn't always show up."

It was a question born of ignorance but we asked him if he had ever married.

"Married? certainly I was married: I was married—four children and eleven grandchildren."

A young lady returning to Hollins once remarked: "Julius Caesar! Aren't you dead yet?"

Remembering that it was decided not to question him at too great a length—the time was growing short—we turned to leave and thanked him for his patience. "If you're going to write me up make it good," he called. "Once somebody wrote something about me in a book: I don't like it and threw 'bout twelve copies in the fire."

We went away thinking that the time was yet far distant when one would come to bury Caesar.[4]

"Was Caesar written about anymore?"

"Child, ol' Caesar was probably in the papers more than anybody around here. Even in the *New York Times* when he died."

Valued Servant at Hollins Dies

Caesar Morton Connected with College Since First Year Lee Surrendered.

Caesar is dead. Caesar Morton, a well beloved colored man, has been connected with the oldest college for women in the oldest state since 1865, or as he expressed it, "ever since de fus' year Lee surrendered." Wherever and whenever Hollins people meet Hollins alumnae and even casual visitors, the question usually comes and comes quickly: "And how is Caesar?" The secret of his amazing popularity was his abounding interest in other people, his unfailing good humor and his own—his very own—smart, quaint and penetrating ways of expressing himself.

William Jennings Bryan was frequently a visitor at Hollins College when his daughter, Miss Grace Bryan, was a student here. On his first visit Caesar waited on Mr. Bryan in the dining room. As the party was leaving the room Caesar joined it and followed Mr. Bryan to the front porch and said: "Mr. Lucian, introduce me to Mr. Bryan." That was quickly and cordially done and a short conversation followed. Mr. Bryan graciously chatted with Caesar, laughed heartily at some of his "wise cracks" and said, "Good-bye." But it was not goodbye yet—for Caesar was holding the then candidate's hand and with an irresistible chuckle said: "Ah—I show is glad I's done shuck han's with one president."

For many years Caesar was a waiter, for many years the head waiter in the college dining room. He had picked up a few French expressions, which somehow always seemed to fit, and he delighted in springing them on the guests at the table. Looking quite serious and solemn, just as if it were his own language, he would say: "Miss, shav lait or l'eau?" When the guest had sufficiently recovered to answer in English, Caesar would say: "tres bein" and go chuckling to the kitchen.

In later years he was retired from active service and rather promoted to the position of "office boy" in the business offices. He was in fact the host in the business office—and nobody was overlooked though everybody was looked over by him. There was in the office some years ago a girl who did some of the clerical work, worked at times on the switchboard, etc. She was limited in experience and in background and none knew that better than Caesar. One morning Caesar was to deliver a message to the librarian. As he started out the girl referred to, said: "Caesar, ask Miss Marian to send me a book." There was something in her tone that Caesar did not like, but he delivered the message promptly. The librarian said: "All right Caesar, what book would you suggest?" And quick as a flash came back the answer: "Send her de *Pilgrim's Progress*."

An old Hollins girl returned to Hollins after a lapse of years. She, of course, chatted with Caesar, teased him a little about sitting around and doing nothing and finally said: "Caesar—I just don't believe it's you—aren't you dead yet?" "Nor'm I ain't dead yet—ain't you married yet?"

But alas! Caesar is dead, but the affection and understanding and sympathetic appreciation of thousands of Hollins girls and visitors still live.

Caesar Morton was born about 1848. He died April 6, 1929. He was one of the three oldest colored men employed at Hollins College. Clem Bolden, who passed away in February, has worked at Hollins since 1865, and Prince Smith, who is still in active service, has been connected with the college since 1873.[5]

Old "Befor' The Wah" Darky Dies at Hollins College

Caesar Morton, a Waiter Since 1865—"Sence de Fus' Year Lee Surrendahed"

The picturesque old servants of the South, the "befo' the wah" darkies, are fast dying out. Many of them well remember their days of slavery, some can tell thrilling tales of Civil War battles.

Caesar Morton, a widely known character throughout Virginia, died recently at Hollins College, where he had lived and been employed since 1865 or, as he expressed it, "ever sence de fus' yeah Lee surrendahed." He was long a waiter in the dining room and was later given odd jobs to do around the business office of the college. Students crossing the campus would find time to stop and ask Caesar's opinion of the weather, of which he was a never-failing prophet, or to listen to his comments. His remarks were sure to be apt and amazingly to the point, so that Caesar's sayings were widely known.

The old colored man was possessed of an unfailing good humor. He picked up a few French expressions which he delighted in springing on guests in the dining room.

An alumna, returning to Hollins after several years, teased Caesar about sitting around and doing nothing, and finally said, "Caesar, I just don't believe it's you—aren't you dead yet?" To which the old man replied: "No-m, I ain't dead yet—ain't you married yet?"

Nothing could compare with Caesar's pride over knowing William Jennings Bryan. Bryan was often a visitor at the college while his daughter was a student there. On his first visit, Caesar waited on Mr. Bryan. As the party was leaving after the meal, Caesar followed and asked to be introduced to Mr. Bryan, who, apprised of the affectionate regard for the old colored man, graciously chatted with him and laughed heartily at some of Caesar's remarks. When he said good-bye, Caesar clung fast to the then candidate's hand and with an irresistible chuckle said: "Ah—I sho is glad I'se shuk han's with one President."[6]

One note I discovered in the "Servants" box, labeled "Memoranda," provides information on Betty Jones Morton, Caesar's wife:

Betty Jones Morton came to Hollins Institute with Dr. & Mrs. John Tompkins from Buckingham Co., Va. Dr. Tompkins' aunt, Miss Betty Jones, for whom Betty Jones Morton was named, gave her to Mrs. Tompkins; she came to Hollins when she was 14, there nursed Leila Turner, daughter of Prof. & Mrs. J. A. Turner, and at 16 married Caesar Morton. Mr. & Mrs. Turner helped to get her ready for the wedding and dress her.

Table 2 The Family of Caesar and Betty Morton

Births

William Criselte Morton	Sept. 15, 1873
Lillie Watson Morton	Sept. 7, 1875
Gertrude Eva Morton	Oct. 7, 1878
Infant (three days old)	Oct. 1882
Grace Ellen Morton	Oct. 7, 1887
John Tompkins Morton	Jan. 7, 1889
Margie Morton	Mar. 7, 1892
Leila Morton	Dec. 4, 1900

Marriages

William Criselte Morton and Molly Fox, Collans Manor, N.Y., 1905
Lillie Watson Morton and John King, Hollins, Va., Oct. 1906
Grace Ellen Morton and George Meade, Hollins, Va., June 1909

Deaths

Gertrude Eva Morton	June 20, 1886
Infant (three days old)	Oct. 1882
John Tompkins Morton	Mar. 1919
Margie Morton	Mar. 5, 1912

I discovered this letter in the box in the library basement.

August 21, 1929

Miss McKinney:

Emily Penick has a picture of Caesar. I think it ought to be preserved. She said she has lost the film. Its a picture of Caesar in a rather interesting position and Penick says that before she took the picture Caesar said, "Oh Lord, give me blue eyes and golden curls." The pose and the remark is so entirely characteristic of Caesar that I thought it would be a good idea to have a small cut made of this picture and a brief paragraph by Penick. She could put that quotation right under the picture and write in one paragraph a few words about Caesar.

If you think well of the suggestion take it up with Emily Penick early in the fall and borrow the picture from her. You will have to be careful to return it to her.

Sincerely,

Jos. A. Turner, Secretary
Hollins College Corporation.

JAT:B

An older Caesar Morton, near East Building (left) and Bradley Hall (right). Hollins Archives.

I read and reread the articles many times, and I tried to remember that in 1927 the Roanoke Times was a small newspaper serving an area in the South that had become middle class because of the Virginia and Tennessee Railroad in 1892. Social and political views were conservative then. During my stay in Roanoke from 1989 to 1993, I found the region still to be conservative, and passive with regard to civil rights. Yet in their time, the articles about Caesar were perhaps considered liberal by the mere fact that so much space was given to a black man. I am sure that Mr. Morton would have been tickled to see so much coverage on him as well. I reminded myself that the jobs at Hollins, particularly the male jobs, were good for their time, and that men like Mr. Morton were proud of their work at the college.

I wondered about Mr. Morton's life outside of Hollins. His family, his children and grandchildren? His dreams for them? What did he think about the changes in the world? When did he first see a car or an airplane? Had he ever spoken on a telephone?

I was saddened by the fact that here was a man who loved education and toiled graciously for sixty-seven years in an educational institution, which was considered the finest of its time, and it didn't occur to one person to recognize that he or any members of his family were capable of learning. The fact that he picked up a few French phrases surprised and delighted everyone. With a little direction he could have learned so much more.

But there was another irony about how Mr. Morton presented himself as the stereotypical "darkie" of the South. I believe that he knew exactly what he was doing, and that he used that presentation as a way of surviving. He reminded me of the trickster character that Frederick Douglass wrote about in his slave narratives, or the familiar Brer Rabbit of Joel Chandler Harris's stories—amusing the boss was the only safe way of getting any personal attention. Caesar Morton knew this well.

3

I Saw Lee Surrender

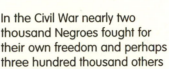

In the Civil War nearly two
thousand Negroes fought for
their own freedom and perhaps
three hundred thousand others
helped as laborers and servants
so that their freedom was not
given to them, but earned.

W. E. B. Du Bois

I had received permission from my advisor that my research on the Hollins Community could be an independent study class for my last semester. I was elated. But then the question was, what do I do next? I started a file system and purchased a cassette player. Every time I spoke with anyone I recorded the conversation, if there were no objections. I talked to anyone who was suggested to me. I was also busy learning about the history of slavery and the Roanoke area. I joined the Roanoke Historical Society, where many of the members were Hollins alumnae.

My next interview with Mrs. Bruce was on a cold bright February afternoon. She said she was "perky and feeling just fine." I decided to ask her out to lunch this time. We dined at the French Asian Cafe, a cozy restaurant in downtown Roanoke. "I'm just tickled pink to be eating out," she said when we arrived at the restaurant.

Nelson Mandela had just been released from prison after twenty-seven years. A feeling of hope energized the air. I had just received an e-mail from my friend Opal Moore, who was in Germany on a Fulbright fellowship. She told me how lonely she felt because now, at one of the most exciting times in history (our history for sure), there was no one to share her joy with. The Germans weren't dancing in the streets for the freedom of Nelson Mandela. I suggested that she write a poem. When Mandela was elected president, Opal composed the following.

the day nelson mandela is voted president

the day nelson mandela is voted president
of south africa
i am standing in a village

31

in germany and i hear from cnn that
the african people are in the streets
singing a song of one word:
mandela mandela mandela

i imagine that every black soul
everywhere is singing and i
listen to the silence across germany
and glance through cynical british
newspapers hinting failure
in between their lines

and i want to sing a song
unconditional because the heart
sometimes wants no conditions
and my ears are full
of the silence of a tongue
I do not speak and cannot hear
and i taste a disciplined indifference
in this silence and

certainly there are no banners waving
so i imagine that someplace in america
there is singing and people
are filing into churches
and standing in the streets
on sidewalks in chicago
and new york and detroit
and l.a. in short everywhere
to watch the news on multiple screens
in cason pirie scot windows on state street or
in the showroom of audiovideo warehouses
in short, the everywhere
of my stranded imagination,

and everywhere
there is this african voice singing
singing south africa's song made of
one word (**mandela mandela mandela**)
an everywhere that does not reach this
german village where silence rises like mist
along those ancient cobbled streets,
slips along the narrow crooked lanes
of germersheim,

a rising silence of dismay?
could it be the dismal
fog of this history must yield
finally to the sunlight
in a black man's face?

—Opal J. Moore (1994)

It was indeed an exciting time in America. The world had changed. Other friends telephoned from all over the world to talk about it. We wanted to remember the moment forever. The sun shined brightly most of that February.

⌒

"I never thought I'd live to see the day that Nelson Mandela would be a free man," I said to Mrs. Bruce.

"What do you mean, Child? I'm the one to who should be saying that."

I smiled and nodded my head in agreement. After the waiter took our orders, I turned to Mrs. Bruce and announced, "I want to know more about your job in the science laboratories."

"Primarily, I was in charge of maintaining and setting up equipment and chemicals for science lab."

"Did you have other responsibilities?"

"All of the blacks were assigned to other work as needed. I was expected to work in the dormitories and other departments during school vacation and while other workers were doing other jobs."

"Did you prefer the chemical laboratories?"

"I sure did. It was a different world. Black folks are supposed to know about cleaning."

"What else did you do in the chemical labs?"

"I took the exams most of the time with the students."

"Was the professor aware of this?"

"Probably not; when he gave tests, he usually left me in charge."

"Where did he go?"

"I don't know," Mrs. Bruce laughed.

"What did you score on the exams?"

"Child, I made a hundred every time except once, when I made only ninety-six."

"Would you like to have been a scientist?"

"I don't know what a scientist does, but I sure loved being in that lab figuring out stuff in those glass containers. They sparkled after I washed them."

"What other kinds of things did you do?"

Before Mrs. Bruce could answer, the waiter appeared with our food. We held hands and Mrs. Bruce said grace.

"I'm starved," I tore into my salad. "You know I haven't had a good tomato in a long time."

"Too much rain. But that reminds me, Miss Smith—"

I cut her off, "Remember our deal: I'm Ethel."

Mrs. Bruce giggled. The expression on her face reminded me of a child's awe, like saying a parent's name for the first time other than Mama and Papa.

"Okay. But I was about to tell you about the time we planted tomatoes on top of the roof."

"Was this in one of your science classes?"

"Sure was. It all started on a Monday morning. The professor was often absent on Monday mornings."

"How come?"

"I don't know. We didn't ask questions. We just did what we were told."

"Please tell me about the tomatoes."

"I found the seeds while I was cleaning one of the cabinet drawers. That was my job as well, to keep everything in order. One of the students suggested that we ought to plant the seeds and hide them, and after they germinated we'd put them on top of the roof, where no one would see them. So we did."

"How many seeds did you plant?"

"About three packs. The trick was that I had put them in a place where the professor would never look. It wasn't that hard since he didn't do much poking around anyway when he was there. He always asked for everything that he needed."

"What did he do when you weren't there?"

"I never missed work. Anyway, we all came in a little early one Monday morning so we could replant the tomatoes and put them on top of the roof. After that I had to remember to water them. Tomatoes need a lot of water and sunshine."

"Then what happened?"

The waiter appeared with a dessert tray. "What's your pleasure, ladies?"

"Help yourself, Mrs. Bruce. They all look good, but I believe I"m going to have the lemon tart."

"That German chocolate cake looks pretty good to me," Mrs. Bruce pointed to her selection.

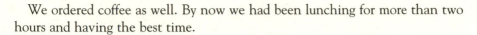

We ordered coffee as well. By now we had been lunching for more than two hours and having the best time.

"Now back to the tomatoes."

"Near the end of the school term, we had the best tomatoes I ever tasted. Big, round, and juicy. I can't remember ever tasting more flavorful tomatoes."

"I wish I had one now," I laughed.

"I love them ripe off the vine. Just a speck of salt and pepper."

"My mother and grandmother canned tomatoes all summer long. Our house was always hot. But we sure were happy in the winter."

"I know what you mean. Canned tomatoes can perk up the poorest meal. I always had a pot of something or other on the stove. In the winter it was likely to be soup. Folks always knew that they could drop by and eat. When the pot got low, I'd throw in a jar of canned tomatoes, and we'd keep right on eating."

"Do you still do that?"

"No, child. I don't do much cooking. No need to with all of the restaurants and such."

"Tell me about some of the others from the community whom you remember as a child, or remember hearing your parents or grandparents speak about."

"Clement Read Bolden was the oldest of all of the men, and around Hollins, as he got older, was called Uncle Clem."

"Do you remember anything else about him?"

"Clem didn't like being cooped up inside with all those clothes on. He wanted to be outside working the grounds. He loved flowers and all of nature. Couldn't read or write much, but knew the seeding, planting, and gathering times better than anyone, even some of the professors, who had studied about land. They were always asking Clem for advice.

"His big day came when, in 1863, he, along with a number of other young colored men, was drafted into the Confederate army. He served two years as a teamster:

> Them dead bodies started smellin.' Us colored men had to bury them fast as we could. Sometimes the ground be hard and cold and diggin' took all of our strength. But with the help of the Good Lord, we got them buried, but there was always more bodies to bury. Couldn't bury no coloreds near the whites. You get beat if you did. Longest two years of my life. Just wanted to get back home to see the flowers growing and blooming. The smell of death was enough to make anyone want to get back to livin."

"How do you know this story?" I asked Mrs. Bruce.

"Uncle Clem was about the age of my grandpapa. Everyone was proud of Clem. Plenty other men from here went to that war too, but Clem could tell stories to hold your attention."

"Did your grandpapa go to war?"

"No, he was too sickly. But he loved Uncle Clem's stories because he could make you feel like you were right there," Mrs. Bruce repeated: "'I was about seventeen years old. Had worked all my life and wasn't scare of no work. But that war near 'bout worked me to death. Worst part, never got no sleep. Had to be on the look-out for them Yankees,'—were other parts of Uncle Clem's account of the war, according to my grandpapa."

Mr. Clem Bolden quickly became a war hero for me. When I found his photographs, I knew that I would never think of the Civil War again without thinking of him. So many black men had fought and aided in the war. Then I wondered if he had been scared. He probably was, never having being away from the college since he had arrived there as a small child. He was probably excited about going into the unknown world of battle. And I am sure that he knew what the war was about, or what it came to be about.

Later, I wondered if maybe the war hadn't meant anything special to him, since he was doing simply what he was told to do. A fact surfaced for me: No wonder so few members of the community were willing to talk to me; they were not used to anyone being interested in them, other than their service. Asking questions and offering opinions weren't in their experience. Again, the slave mentality of silence persisted in the community and at the college.

Around the same time that I discovered Mr. Bolden's story, Ken Burns, the documentary filmmaker, had produced a series on the Civil War. I anxiously awaited its showing. I wanted to place Mr. Clem Bolden right there.

I found this document in the box marked "Servants" in the basement of the library. It is written just as I found it. No author was mentioned.

After the War Uncle Clem returned to Hollins and was in continuous service there until he died. His longest service was that as head gardener. "I used to dream about the beautiful flowers at Hollins College, especially when the weather warmed up," Clem told folks.

In January, 1925, Uncle Clem appeared one morning in the office of Mr. Joseph Turner, the business manager of Hollins College, and handed him a clipping from a Richmond newspaper. He said: "Mr. Turner can't you get one of them things?" The news articles told of a colored man in Salem, Virginia, who had gotten a Confederate pension by reason of his service in the Confederate Army as a body servant.

Mr. Turner made every effort to get some record of Clem Bolden's service, but was unsuccessful in finding any recorded facts. Finally, he sent for Uncle Clem and had him to tell his own story.[1]

Statement made by Clem Bolden and taken down by Jos. A. Turner. January 30, 1928.

I was born in Henrico and belonged to [the] estate of Mrs. Clem Read. (Mr. Clem Read was father to Mr. Tom and David Read.)

When I was a very little boy I came to Mr. David Read's place in Roanoke County. Mr. Charles L. Cocke hired my father and mother and family sometime before the war. (About 1857.)

I waited on table[s] in [the] dining room [at Hollins]. Mr. Dick Walrond came here in Fall of 1863 and everybody he put his hand on had to go.

I got on [the] train at Salem and went down about Petersburg and Richmond. Then we walked to a place called Dutch Gap.

We was on one side of the river and the Yankees was on [the] other side. They was shooting at us all the time. We could see the big cannon balls and dodge 'em, but we couldn't dodge the bullets.

I drove a wagon all over Lunenburg and Mecklenburg and all up around Keysville and Burkville Junction. Sometimes we would stay out three weeks.

I drove a wagon to Appomattox and was there at the surrender. A lot of 'em runned away but I didn't know where to go. I was there about three weeks loading up guns and things. Guns was stacked same as wheat in harvest.

Then we went to Richmond and I was there about two months watering the horses and mules and doing things like that. Then I went to the Capitol Square and they give me a free pass back home and I got off [the] train at Bonsacks.

I come right here to work for Mr. Cocke and I been here ever since.

Note: The above statement is so evidently true that Clem Bolden was awarded the pension he sought. It is interesting to note that he has recited the facts in chronological order. He mentions Burkville Junction. The Junction was dropped from the name of that station many years ago. He also mentions Lunenburg, Mecklenburg, and Keysville—names which he has probably not heard since the Civil War.

According to deed books of Roanoke County, Clem Bolden purchased ten acres of land from the Moores (a prominent family) for one hundred dollars in 1908.

The following obituary was written by Joseph A. Turner, who for eighteen months had written letters to the Veterans' Department on the behalf of Mr. Bolden, eventually procuring twenty-five dollars for him.

Clem Bolden was born about 1846, [and] died February 19, 1929. In 1857 Charles L. Cocke, of Hollins College, hired from David Read, of Monterey, James (Uncle Jim) and Amanda (Aunt Mandy) Bolden, and all their large family of children. Among these children was Clement Read Bolden, afterwards known as "Uncle Clem."

Clem Bolden.
Hollins Archives.

As a boy Clem worked at Hollins in various capacities and in the year of 1863 Clem, along with a number of other young colored men, was drafted into the Confederate Army and served two years as a teamster.

After the War he returned to Hollins and has been in continuous service there ever since. His longest service was that of head gardener. Although he could neither read nor write he knew the varieties and quantities of the seeds and plants he wanted; he knew the seeding, planting and gathering times and he was a good gardener. As his years advanced he was given much lighter work and for many years he worked with the shrubs and flowers on the Hollins College campus, and picked up papers and "odds and ends." To say that he was regular, systematic, conscientious and loyal states the simple facts. Furthermore, he was an interesting character, a fine weather prophet and quite a philosopher. We shall not see his like again. He seldom used his "off days" and he never had to be reminded of any work he had been told to do.

Until about the middle of January, 1929, he did his daily tasks—then he was taken sick and a few weeks later he died.

Table 3 Family Members of Clem Bolden

R. R. Bolden	b. Apr. 12, 1888; d. Sept. 12, 1948
Robert Lewis Bolden	b. June 30, 1910; d. Nov. 16, 1968
Malinda Bolden	in 1900 spent $10 for 130 poles of W. G. Nininger's land*
Rosa Bolden (Big Rosa)	
Carter Bolden	

*W. G. Nininger was a local white merchant, who, according to Mrs. Bruce, owned much of the land in the Hollins Community area.

The following letters from Hollins officials and government representatives tell the story of Clem Bolden's struggle to receive a pension.

September 11, 1924

Mr. John H. Johnson
Pension Department
Richmond, Va.

Dear Sir:

Clem Bolden, a colored man who has worked for us practically all of his life, has called my attention to an article under the Richmond date line of August 29 in regard to colored men who worked on the battlefields during the Civil War.

Uncle Clem has considerable information in his head as to his record but I do not know that he can establish any actual proof. He wants me to find out whether what he can offer is sufficient.

A rough outline of his record is as follows: Clem Bolden belonged to Mr. David Read, who lived about five miles from "Hollins Institute." Charles L. Cocke, my grandfather, hired Clem as a boy in his teens from Mr. David Reed and for sometime during the war Clem worked regularly here. In 1864 he was drafted and the officers came for him here. He left with them and was with the Army until the close of the War. He says that he was in Poages Battaline, that he was sent first to Richmond and immediately from Richmond to a place called Dutch Gap, between Richmond and Petersburg. He says further that the Yankees were digging at that point and that there was some fighting every day

Clem Bolden. Hollins Archives.

between the Yankees, on one side of the river, and our "men on dis" side of the river. Clem drove a wagon. He says that the men found out that they could dodge the big balls because they could see them coming; they could not dodge the little balls because of not being able to see them. Clem says that he was fired on many [times.]

[Apparently the second page of this letter is missing; see, however, the note by Matty Cocke of October 15, 1924.]

Commonwealth of Virginia
Auditor of Public Accounts
Richmond
September 15, 1924

Mr. Joseph Turner,
General Manager,
Hollins, Virginia.

Mr dear Sir:

Answering your letter of recent date, asking about a pension for a colored man by the name of Clem Bolden, I beg to state that we will send you a blank form for him to make application on, as soon as we get a new supply from the printer.

I suggest that every effort be made to prove his service by one or two persons having personal knowledge of such.

Yours very truly,

Jno H. Johnson
PENSION CLERK.

JHJ/s

October 15, 1924

Clem Bolden says that after the fall of Richmond and Petersburg, he drove one of many army wagons (with two mules) to Appomattox, reaching there Sunday, April 9, 1865. He remembers that he was standing near the place where General Lee surrendered to General Grant. After this they returned to a point between Petersburg and Richmond, and was employed several weeks there in removing ammunition, etc.

After almost a month, they were ordered to the Capitol Square in Richmond, and were discharged with transportation papers via packet boat from Richmond to Lynchburg, and then by train.

Clem does not remember the date of his arrival here. He talks intelligently about conditions, and I believe his word may be relied on.

Matty L. Cocke.

January 13, 1925.

Mr. B. O. James
Security of Commonwealth
Richmond, Va.

Dear Sir:

Sometime ago Clem Bolden, colored, asked us to make application for him for a pension. Clem was a slave. He belonged to Mr. David Reed of Roanoke County. He was hired by Mr. David Read to Charles L. Cocke. He was drafted into the Army and left Hollins the day after he received notice. He served as a driver from the time that he was drafted—sometime in 1863, I believe—until the surrender. He was present at the surrender.

I took this matter up by correspondence with somebody in Richmond. My recollection is that I would be furnished with a special form to be filled out by Clem Bolden and that this form was to be accompanied by letters and affidavits from reliable witnesses. This form has never been supplied. This matter escaped my mind and I am not now able to locate in the files the name of the party with whom I had the correspondence.

I would appreciate very much your telling me to whom I should write in behalf of Clem Bolden.

Thanking you, I am

Very truly yours,

Jos. A. Turner,
General Manager.

JAT:B

January 13, 1925

Mr. C. D. Denit, Clerk,
Salem, Va.

Dear Mr. Denit:

I want you to do something for an old Confederate Veteran.

Clem Bolden, colored, was a slave that belonged to Mr. David Read of Roanoke County. He was hired by David Read to Charles L. Cocke. He worked at Hollins as a waiter in the dining room. Sometimes during the year 1863 (Clem thinks it was fall of '63), an officer, R. L. Walrond, called Hollins and served notice on Clem that he had been drafted into the Army. Clem says that whoever "Mr. Dick" Walrond put his hands on had to go. Clem left the next day and served as a driver from that date until the surrender. He served in and around Richmond and drove his team all over the adjoining counties for forage and supplies.

Some years ago I was looking over some records in Botetourt County and noticed that there were some records in regard to slaves who were drafted for the Army. It occurs to me that there may be some similar record in Roanoke County. I would appreciate your advising me whether there is such a record, whether you can find Clem Bolden's name and whether you can find any record in regard to the slaves of David Reid being drafted for the Army.

With good wishes, I am

                                        Sincerely yours,

                                        Jos. A. Turner

JAT:B

                                        Office of Clerk of Roanoke County
                                        Salem, Virginia
                                        January 22, 1925

Joseph A. Turner, Esq.,
Hollins, Va.

Dear Mr. Turner,

I have your favors concerning "Uncle" Clem Bolden, and wish I could help you in assisting to get him the pension desired. I cannot find any records here, however, concerning him or his services. I think, however, that if he can establish, by competent witnesses, his services you refer to, there must be a way to grant him his pension. Several colored men from this County have secured pensions as laborers on breast-works, body servants &c., and I think the law is elastic enough to cover Clem Bolden's case, provided he can establish his claim, as the law and the Auditor construe it. At present I have no access to the form of application, but the certificates required will show what is necessary to be done. If he can get the necessary witnesses, the endorsement of the local Camp and Pension board, I am sure the Court would approve it. Then the necessary order would be entered here, and the papers forwarded to the Auditor. That is all the Clerk can do in these matters.

Sorry I cannot be of more assistance to you.

                                        Yours very truly,

                                        Charles D. Denit, Clerk.

January 23, 1925.

Mr. Frank W. Read
Roanoke, Virginia

Dear Frank:

I have been trying to gather information in regard to Clem Bolden, colored, who is making application for a pension on account of service in the Confederate Army.

Uncle Clem tells a very straight story and I am perfectly certain that he rendered the services. However, we have no actual proofs. It occurs to me that you may have some record.

Clem was born on your grandfather's estate in Henrico County. He belonged to Mrs. Clem Read. Prior to the War and when he was quite a small boy his father, mother and children came to this county. Charles L. Cocke hired James Bolden, Mandy Bolden, his wife and all of their children from your father. Clem as a boy in his teens was a waiter in the dining room. He was drafted into the Army and in the Fall of 1863 he went in as a teamster.

Have you any records of the slaves who were drafted from your father's estate and if so can you find in that record Clem Bolden's name?

With good wishes, I am

Sincerely yours,

Jos. A. Turner.

JAT:B

Office of Clerk of Roanoke County
Salem, Virginia
Feb. 2, 1925.

Joseph A. Turner, Esq.,
Hollins Institute,
Virginia

My dear Mr Turner,

I have your favor of 31st inst., enclosing pension blank of "Uncle" Clem Bolden. I will have pleasure in laying it before the Court when it meets, and have also called attention to the Chairman of the Pension Board that it has been filled and asked them to approve it. As soon as it is completed, I will gladly forward to the Auditor of Public Accounts, to whom it must go for final action.

With best wishes, I am

Yours very truly,

Charles D. Denit,
Clerk.

Hollins College
Hollins, Virginia
Office of General Manager
March 11, 1929.

Mr. Jno H. Johnson, Pension Clerk,
Comptroller's Office,
Richmond, Va.

Dear Sir:

Before filling out the form recently received in connection with the allowance due to the estate of Clem Bolden, please advise me whether I can qualify to receive this money for Clem's estate or whether his daughter will have to qualify.

Clem's widow is a very old woman and is quite ill at this time. It is rather difficult for his daughter to go to Salem to see about this matter. I will be very glad to handle it for her, thus saving time and trouble. I wanted, however, to find out whether that was permissible.

I am today writing to the undertaker requesting a duplicate copy of his bill, together with a copy of his death certificate.

Awaiting your advice, I am

Very truly yours,

Jos. A. Turner
General Manager.

JAT:B

[Response, typed at bottom of the same letter:]

Either you can qualify on the estate of Clem R. Bolden, or any of his family by arranging with the clerk of the court for the purpose of collecting the funeral expense allowance.

John H. Johnson.
Pension Clerk.

March 19, 1929.

Mr. Glenn Murray,
Hollins, Va.

Dear Glenn:

I hand you herewith papers which I am filling in order to collect a $25.00 claim for the estate of Clem Bolden.

Kindly acknowledge my signature. You will note that no fee is allowed for witnessing signatures in a case like this. After you have acknowledged my signature kindly seal the letter and forward, as directed, to Chas. D. Denit, Clerk, Salem, Va.

Thanking you, I am

Sincerely,

Jos. A. Turner

Encl.
JAT:B

March 19, 1929.

Mr. C. C. Williams, Undertaker,
126 Gilmer Ave., N.W.,
Roanoke, Va.

Dear Sir:

I am informed by the State Pension Department (Confederate) that Clem R. Bolden is entitled to a small allowance on account of his funeral expenses.

In order to collect this allowance for this estate it will be necessary for me to have a duplicate state of your account. Will you kindly send me this at your earliest convenience?

I am making this request with the approval of his daughter, Mrs. Eliza Carrington.

Very truly yours,

Jos. A. Turner,
General Manager.

JAT:B

Clem Bolden.
Hollins Archives.

March 19, 1929.

Mr. Chas. D. Denit, Clerk,
Salem, Va.

Dear Mr. Denit:

Clem R. Bolden, colored, who for several years has received a pension of $25.00 a year on account of service in the Confederate Army, recently died.

I am told by Mr. John H. Johnson, Pension Clerk, Richmond, Va., to whom I sent notice of Clem's death, that is an allowance of $25.00 due the estate of the pensioner for funeral expenses. Mr. Johnson has sent me a blank form which I am handing you herewith. Mr. Johnson tells me, in answer to my inquiry on the subject that either I can qualify on the estate or any member of his family by arranging with the Clerk of the Court for the purpose of collecting the funeral expense allowance.

I am handing you herewith certain documents—certificate and account of funeral expense and duplicate bill for same from the undertaker. On receipt of the $25.00 I will turn over same to the two daughters of the deceased.

Thanking you for your certificate in the case, I am

Very truly yours,

Jos. A. Turner,
General Manager.

Encl.
JAT:B

4

Thursday Afternoons

on thursday afternoons the girls
from oldfield come
to collect the week's wash

on thursday afternoons there is little
doubt as to what the mistress wants

they give on demand
polite and curtsey under
bundles balanced

in heliotroic bouquets
sweat smudges turned to musk

they are necessary
like horses or the four-
in-hand fathers sent

along with petticoats, flat
irons and jasmine soap

they cross the field
stop and move as the day
demands

they are thin trees
elegant and swift

with luck a pair
of new shoes satin
blue black patent

long skirts float
above the marsh grass

but for the girls of hollins
they are no more
than well placed palms shading

than from a slavish
virginia sun

Colleen J. McElroy

Ash trees burst into bloom at the bottom of the Hollins Community, just as they had one year earlier. Boaters headed toward Carvin's Cove for their first spring outings. Mrs. Bruce and the offering of spring encouraged me to go back to the church in spite of my memorable encounter with Reverend Calloway. And I knew that if I had any chance of getting folks to talk to me about the history of the community, then the church had to be a factor. I convinced myself to have hope. And if there were any place I could feel at home, it should be a Southern Baptist church: A Southern Baptist black church in Alabama is like a Southern Baptist black church in Virginia—or anywhere else in the South.

Once there, in terms of the church service, I felt at home. The smell of fried chicken and potato salad still reeked through the thin walls. The ceiling fans spread hot air to the sweating congregation. Everyone participated. If you knew the songs, you sang; and if you didn't, you clapped, patted, or even stomped. Babies cried as the piano and organ hummed loudly. After that Sunday I didn't feel like an outsider. I returned to the church many times. Members grew used to seeing me there. They still didn't talk to me, but they occasionally nodded their heads in my direction.

In my American literature class at Virginia Tech, I taught Mark Twain's essay "A War Prayer," trying to make sense out of the Gulf War. I thought discourse with my students would help; it had in the past, at times. America's aggression had been necessary in order to "create a new world order," claimed our President.

I raised the same question to my students as Twain did in his essay. "When there's a war, whose side is God on?" Most of my students immediately responded without thinking: "on our side." Others said nothing. I asked my students: "What about the people on the other side? Were they simply born in the wrong place or at the wrong time? Who was their God?" Class was painful and difficult for me that day. I couldn't generate an intellectual discussion around issues of ethics, principles, or even hope, as far as that was concerned. I was too emotional to press harder. Major mistake.

I dismissed my class early. I drove home to Roanoke with no plans; I only knew that it was too early to crawl into bed and cry. I returned to the Fishburn Library at Hollins College to spend more time with the 1903 Spinster, where I had discovered the photographs of women walking to the spring with baskets of laundry on their heads.

I struggled to understand this custom of the women dressing up in their best Sunday clothes to perform the task of laundry. From Mrs. Bruce, I learned that after washing the clothes at the spring, they hung them on a wire fence. When the clothes dried, they carried them to their homes and ironed them with heavy starch and then returned them to their owners.

One of the photographs said it all, the one of the women carrying the baskets of laundry on their heads. The image made me wonder if these women were aware of the timelessness of the custom, its antiquity. Yet these were women of the twentieth century. Another photo showed a young girl with happy and proud eyes; as I tried to calculate her age, I wondered what she would think today if she knew that I was trying to piece together her life and write about her and her world. Would it matter to her? I wanted to know more than just what she did. That part of her life was clear by looking at the photographs. I wanted to know her unvoiced thoughts and dreams. What did she like to eat? Where did they get her dress-up dress from for the Thursday afternoons? How was she treated by her mistresses? Who were her people? Was she told stories of life before the college? Did she piece quilts like my mother and grandmother and all of the women in my family before them? Did she can fruits and vegetables in the summer? Did she love flowers like me?

I estimated that the young girl in the photograph would be about the same age today that my grandmother would have been—ninety. I had never seen a photograph of my grandmother as a little girl, nor had I ever imagined her being a little girl. I showed the photographs to Mrs. Bruce.

Unidentified "washerwoman"; Oldfield and Tinker Mountain in background. *The Spinster*, 1903, p. 34.

Unidentified "washerwoman"; West Building in background.
The Spinster, 1903, p. 33.

"Do you recognize any of the women in the photographs?"

"No, I don't, but it was a common sight around here. Mama used to do laundry, but she wasn't one of the washerwomen who dressed up like the ones in the photographs. But that's why the pictures were in the Spinster. Everyone, at least the ones close to my age, remembers being told about them," Mrs. Bruce laughed.

"Do you remember the names of any of the women told to you?"

"They were just called washerwomen. You can imagine that they washed all of the bed linens, table linens, laundry for the students, as well as laundry for members of the Cocke, Turner, and Pleasants families. So they must have been busy all the time. It was just on Thursday afternoon that they washed for their mistresses or the students."

"Did anyone else in your family ever wash clothes?" I asked.

"Mama took in washing. It allowed her to stay at home, since it was eight of us children, and earn a little money at the same time."

"Do you remember when the women stopped carrying the baskets on their heads?" I asked.

Mrs. Bruce cocked her head back. She always made this gesture when she was trying to recall a specific fact. And like a computer, an answer appeared. "Probably around the 1930s or 1940s."

"Why then?"

The deaths of Charles Lewis Cocke, Susanna Pleasants Cocke, William Pleasants, Joseph Turner, and Miss Matty Cocke had removed some of the last vestiges of the work relations that initially characterized the college.

Clem Bolden and the other old-timers like Caesar Morton had died, and so had the Charles Lewis Corporation—but the Hollins College Corporation was created in its place. The transfer to public ownership was completed on August 1, 1932. As the proprietary institution and many of its founders passed on, workers would have to perform their duties without relying upon random instructions from various supervisors, like Mr. Bolden and Mr. Morton had for more than fifty years. For the first time, members of the Hollins Community would work for a new supervisor instead of a member of the Cocke, Pleasants, or Turner families.[1]

"Did folks in the community speak of this change?" I asked Mrs. Bruce.

"I don't know that much. By then I was living in Roanoke going to high school."

"Do you think folks were scared of losing their jobs?"

"Probably not; there is always work in service for black folks. Some may have been concerned about who they would work for, and hoped the person would be good to them. Or at least as good as they had been treated before."

"Were some employers better than others?"

"Sure. But I am not calling any names," Mrs. Bruce laughed. "I never heard tell of anyone just being plain mean to folks. Everyone knew everyone and everyone's family. But some folks were just easier to get along with than others, if you know what I mean." Mrs. Bruce continued.

Under the presidency of Bessie Carter Randolph, plans were made to expand enrollment, gain accreditation, and modernize operations. Laundry was a large

Unidentified "washerwoman"; Oldfield and Tinker Mountain
in background. *The Spinster*, 1903, p. 34.

part of that modernization. Steam washing machines were first installed in 1939 behind Botetourt Hall to handle the institutional laundry. Until then, the women in the community had done all the laundry, institutional as well as that of the students, and sometimes the clothing of the staff and faculty. It was not until the early 1950s, when laundry facilities were constructed for student use, that the women finally stopped carrying the baskets of laundry on their heads.2

Again, I was haunted with thoughts of my own mother, who spent fifty years cleaning the house of the same white family. My sisters and I knew her only through her work, not words; by touch and silence. When Mother would arrive home from work bone-tired, we soaked her feet in an old tin blue wash pan with hot water and epsom salt. One of my sisters poured the hot water; I massaged her feet, and my younger sister patted them dry. Mother often napped during these sessions. We just performed; we didn't talk because we didn't want to wake her. Mother knew how to lay her head just right on the sofa so we could condition and brush her hair—her long dark curly hair that neither my sisters nor myself inherited.

Our other chores, to help Mother, included sprinkling the starched clothes she took in to iron from another white family for a dollar per laundry basket. After the clothes were sprinkled, we placed them in a plastic bag in the bottom of the refrigerator where they waited for our tired mother in the evenings.

Afterwards we fixed her a plate of whatever Big Mama had cooked. Sometimes we gave her updates on the Perry Mason show from television. Often she fell asleep before we completed the updates. We never got around to our lives at school or church; she was snoring for sure by then.

We were never awarded the house with the screened back porch that was surrounded by oak trees. The Tomblins left no will. But distant relatives showed up to clean the house out, taking every piece of furniture, even the curtains, back with them up north. Nothing was left afterwards. First the house was put up for sale. Then a poor white family rented and trashed it. Once they moved out it was empty. Year after year, we watched the house rot away as we drove by it on the big yellow school bus.

Big Mama was thankful when the house finally fell to the ground. She said she always thought Mother would die from a broken heart. She had believed that the house would be ours one day, and that would make up for all of those Sundays and Christmases she had missed with us.

When I was in high school in the 1960s (I graduated in 1970), my mother was paid fifteen dollars a week by the Tomblins. She earned an additional three to five dollars every other week from ironing. With that she supported me, my two sisters, my grandmother, and herself.

As a child I never understood why my mother had to work on Sundays and Christmases. I knew no else who did. Who were these people, these Tomblins, who couldn't unwrap their store-bought gifts without help? Who couldn't put cooked food on the table? Or wash just a few dishes on the weekends or holidays? Didn't they realize that Mother had a family who needed her? This world of service never made sense to me. It will forever haunt me.

Because Mother was always too exhausted to help us do anything, our grandmother was in charge of domestic relations in our house. My sisters and I were fortunate to have someone to love and care for us. What happened to all of those children who didn't have a grandmother to be in charge of domestic relations? Working with the Hollins Community offered me the gift of being just a little bit more thankful to my own mother.

As my last semester and the program at Hollins College were nearing an end, I knew I had discovered meaningful and valuable work that would always be with me. But I was also aware that I had to learn more about the history of not just slavery, but of the Roanoke Valley. I had begun by joining the Roanoke Historical Society. Then I started a reading list. One of the first books I read was a book about the history of a town near my own hometown in Alabama called Clio, Alabama: A History, by Alto L. Jackson. Immediately, I noticed that the lives of the black citizens, who made up more than half of the population, were not included. The same was true with Hollins College: An Illustrated History, by Frances J. Niederer, with the exception of one page dedicated to Caesar Morton and Lewis Hunt. I was later inspired by the work of David Huddle in Helen Lewis and Suzanna O'Donnell's Remembering Our Past: Building Our Future, which did include black citizens. I then searched for books that would offer me models for what I was trying to do. I found none. Later during the year, We Were Always Free: The Maddens of Culpepper, Virginia was published by one of the Madden children. The book was well received and reviewed. It was the first source to offer me some ideas.

During this time I met Mary Bishop, a reporter for the Roanoke Times. She became a resourceful advisor and a good friend. She was also involved in a project about the Gainesboro Community, which had been a solid, middle-class, African American community until urban renewal looped Highway 581 through the center of it. And by doing so, most of the citizens who had lived there for generations were displaced. We had much to talk about, for she too was a graduate of the Creative Writing Program at Hollins College. She had also been part of a group of reporters who had been awarded a Pulitzer Prize at the Philadelphia Enquirer.

I also met John Kern, a historian and the director of the Virginia Historical and Preservation Society. He taught me how to research data on microfilm in the main library in the city of Roanoke. He prepared a more sophisticated reading list for me on slavery. He believed in my project and was always willing to discuss it with me.

Those women carrying baskets on their heads to the spring were lodged in my memory. I couldn't sleep without seeing them. I wanted them to speak to me, but they would only shake their heads and smile at me in my sleep. I stopped hoping for language from them and decided that I was the student and my job was to learn by whatever means necessary to me. I had their photographs. These women with baskets of laundry on their heads were with me. In spite of them not speaking to me, I felt their presence, especially when I walked around campus trying to piece together the quilt of their lives.

I was also pondering my own life. I had been offered a position as an instructor of English at Virginia Polytechnic State University in Blacksburg, Virginia. The best news would be that I would be working with the renowned poet Nikki Giovanni. I felt like the gates of heaven had just opened up to me. And more importantly, I didn't have to leave Mrs. Bruce. I don't know if I could have, and I feel thankful that I never had to make the decision. She had become more important to me than I realized. I wasn't concerned with the fact that my new job required me to teach four classes a semester—about 150 students—and it paid less than twenty thousand dollars a year. I could continue living in my house in Old Southwest, in Roanoke, without a roommate, and commute to Virginia Tech. The associate chair was sensitive to that fact, particularly when I explained to her that my son had a job at a restaurant in Roanoke when he was home on break, and that my taking the new position was necessary to keep him in college.

Mrs. Bruce was thrilled for me. Her grandson George had earned a football scholarship to Virginia Tech.

With a small grant of three hundred dollars from Hollins College, I was able to get some of the photographs reproduced as slides. I soon began presenting lectures on my ongoing research around the Roanoke area. The level of interest

Women with baskets of laundry.
The Spinster, 1903, p. 31.

from audiences further inspired me. The photographs of the women with the baskets on their heads always evoked the most heartfelt response.

I had been involved in a car accident that winter and was thankful to be alive; I was more determined than ever to give meaning to my work. The work of a community was the work of recording its culture, I believed. I wanted to find out about the culture of the Hollins Community; I wanted the oral stories. I was frustrated because I couldn't find Zora Neale Hurston's Eatonville. The only aspects of Hurston's Eatonville I found was "the tongueless, earless, and eyeless." But I had to remember that the Hollins Community was not the fictional world of Toni Morrison's "bottom" or Ernest Gaines's "quarters." This was real life, and in real life folks—particularly from an oppressed community—didn't have stories from an oral tradition, and if they did, they were buried somewhere deep in the language of silence. But I had Mrs. Bruce, who inspired me to trust my own voice, and that was power. I do believe that most community residents had stories and simply weren't aware of what they had. No one had ever asked them for stories or opinions. They were accustomed to a world of being told what to do without asking questions. The language of silence is such a product of a plantation-rooted system.

But I had the women with the baskets on their heads. I wanted to know them. I kept asking questions. What were their names? I was only able to find the name of one: Malinda Morton, a washerwoman who appeared to be bold enough to regularly request payment in kind. Yet she did so only after 1871.[3]

Another concept bothered me; for not only were the names of the women hidden from me, but there had never been a memorial service for any of them like there had been for Caesar Morton and Lewis Hunt. For instance, what happened to Lewis Hunt's grandmother: Ginnie Hunt, who, as so many have said, was "respected by all who knew her and nursed so many of the babies in the Cocke/Turner family?" Was their work not as valuable? And again—what happened to the no-named, no-narrative women with the baskets on their heads? Would they always dance in my dreams?

5

Dean of Servants

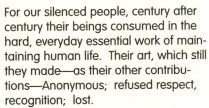

For our silenced people, century after
century their beings consumed in the
hard, everyday essential work of maintaining human life. Their art, which still
they made—as their other contributions—Anonymous; refused respect,
recognition; lost.

Tillie Olsen

On the afternoon that Supreme Justice William Brennan retired, the niece of
Mr. Zachariah Hunt Jr. telephoned to inform me that he had died; they had
known of my work researching the history of the community, and before he died
he had granted me permission to look through his box of old photographs and
other materials, allowing me to keep the items I wanted. I offered her and her
family my sympathy and thanked her for calling. We agreed to meet the following Saturday.

I hardly slept that week thinking of Mr. Hunt, the son of the eldest of Lewis
Hunt's nine children, and how I wished I had known him and could have talked
to him. Despite that sense of personal loss, I was very thankful for his last thoughts.
I called Mrs. Bruce to see if she could join me at Mr. Hunt's house, which was a
stone's throw from her house. As usual, she was delighted and willing.

We arrived at nine o'clock on a sunny spring morning. Redbud bloomed all over
the mountains of Virginia. The first thing I noticed was that Mr. Hunt's house did
not look like the other houses in the community. Today, most of the houses look
like Mrs. Bruce's—ranch-styled brick, built on a government plan called FHA
220. In fact, my mother's house in Alabama is similar. Mr. Hunt's house was a
Victorian-style house off of Reservoir Road in the Cufftown section of the Hollins
Community. The front porch sagged a bit and the house was in need of some basic
repairs, but it was clear that it had been an elegant house. It was so quiet I almost
thought that no one was at home. But soon Ms. Hunt came to the door. After
greeting Mrs. Bruce and me, she invited us in. The inside of the house was very
much like Mrs. Bruce's house, with the exception that there were no flowers or
photographs. The furniture was covered with sheets, making it difficult to guess
about more than its shapes. A glass-doored bureau took up most of the space in

the dining room and a covered table filled the rest. An old mirror hung over the mantle of a brick fireplace. We sat at the dining-room table. Ms. Hunt was a quite soft-spoken young woman who looked toward the floor when she spoke.

"Again, let me express my sympathy to you and your family," I said.

"Thank you," she said without looking up.

"Zack will be missed. That's for sure," Mrs. Bruce said.

"Here's the box," she offered me an old yellowed cardboard box that looked something like a hat box that my grandmother had used.

"Thank you," I accepted nervously. "I'll take care of them and will return them if you like."

"You can keep them. He wanted you to have them. Plus, we don't want them."

"Did he say anything else?" I asked.

"Not that I know of."

When I raised the lid of the box, the swirling dust made us cough. It was the first and only time the young woman smiled.

"It sure was good for Zack to save something of his history," Mrs. Bruce said.

Mrs. Bruce had appeared small and fragile as she put on her large eyeglasses. But to me that day, she was as big as a mountain. I don't know if I would have been able to get through the meeting with Ms. Hunt without her. It wasn't anything Mrs. Bruce said or did in particular; her presence alone offered me courage. Everyone in the community trusted and respected her. She could be counted on as the person who would always help. She can "never sit home for too long on the days that don't belong to the Lord." She not only visited the sick, but she tended to them. She gathered used clothing and sent the summer ones to Africa and the winter ones to the Total Action Project (TAP), a nonprofit service organization in Roanoke. And for herself, she gardened her African violets and played the piano.

This is the first article I found in the box:

Faithful Friend
St. Valentine's Day has always been a special day for Lewis Hunt, for 50 years a waiter at Hollins College—it's his birthday. Students at the College made his 63rd birthday on February 14 especially memorable by presenting him with a gold pocket watch and chain, engraved with his name and the date and inscribed "From the Students" and "50 Years of Faithful Service."

Lewis Hunt receiving gifts during his surprise birthday party on February 14, 1948. Photo from Zackery Hunt; in collection of the author.

Lewis's surprise and pleasure at the unexpected attention showed clearly on his shining face. His sense of the fitness of things was gratified, too, because the student chosen to present the gift was Miss Lyn Neil, a great-granddaughter of the founder and first president, Mr. Charles Lewis Cocke, under whose regime Lewis first came to work on the campus. The last 47 years of Lewis's 50 years at the College have spent as head-waiter.

The presentation was made in the dining hall during the lunch hour. The waiters and waitresses—among them several of Lewis' own children—were present as well as students, faculty, and staff. The seniors sang "Happy Birthday" and the College gave him a handsome tiered cake, aglow with 63 lighted candles.

Lewis is the third generation of his family to serve the College and the Cocke family. His grandmother, Aunt Ginnie Hunt, respected by all who knew her, was the nurse for many years in the family of the late Joseph A. Turner. Lewis himself is the father of nine living children, seven of whom work at the College, and he has 15 grandchildren, one of whom already works there.

Lewis's first job at the College was tending sheep. That was in 1898 when he was a barefoot boy of 13. He had other duties too, among them keeping President Cocke's "fine Morocco boots" clean and gleaming; pumping the organ in the Chapel when "Mr. Fisher" played, and running to the top of Main Building every hour to ring the bell for classes.

When he was called upon to wait on "The Founder's" table, Lewis was still a boy in short trousers. That he did his job even then with natural aplomb seems evident, since when he was 16, "The Founder" chose him for the high position of head waiter. It was then Lewis purchased his first pair of long pants, deeming them essential to the dignity of the position.

Deeply religious, Lewis is a leading member of the Baptist Church, formerly known as the Lovely Zion, in the Hollins community. He says three things always go with him: His Church, his family, and the College. Present at every important occasion at the College for the past 50 years, Lewis could fill two books with his reminiscences, both of the "dark days" in the years of Reconstruction, and of the years of growth and expansion since then.

His dignity is unassailable, his loyalty unquestioning, and his innate courtesy unfailing. His slightest word is law for the other dining room help, perhaps because his sense of justice is as dependable as his word.[1]

Lewis Hunt cutting his cake during his sixty-third birthday. Photo from Zackery Hunt; in collection of the author.

I must have read this article five times when I first discovered it. I read it first for the information, and later for the inside story. It's the story behind the information that interested me. I asked myself, "What is wrong with this article?" I tried very hard not to place it in the context of today, remembering that it was written in 1948, when little regard was given to the language of racism. Indeed, taking that into consideration, it is filled with praise.

I tried to imagine Mr. Hunt as a thirteen-year-old boy in 1898 in short pants, running around the college to ring the bell every hour, shine the boots of the founder, pump the organ, and do whatever else he was told. This would have been exciting for any boy of that age at the turn of the century. The story of Mr. Lewis Hunt's life could be seen as the great American success story, where a member of one generation worked his way up from shining the founder's boots to being headwaiter—"Dean of Servants"—a title he gave himself. He probably came to Hollins College with his grandmother, Mrs. Ginnie Hunt, who came with the Cocke family and was probably enslaved. In fact, his first name bears part of the name of the founder, Charles Lewis Cocke, indicating that there were close family bonds.

But then the dream unravels and turns into an American nightmare for me, as history often does for too many African Americans. Why was it that Hunt's wife couldn't have been mentioned by name in the article? Particularly since the writer herself notes how important his family was to him. And what about his nine children? Why was it they couldn't obtain an education that would at least enable them to attain a status equal to that of their father's? What about the fifteen grandchildren? Not one of their names is mentioned in the article, either, only the proud fact that one of them already worked at the college. Their work at the college should have been an improvement from their father's. But such attainment is not possible when the work continues to be in service, generation after generation. History repeated itself. What kind of future did the college offer to these founding members?

For a family to continue in a line of service work is not progress. In fact, in this case I believe it was a regression. When Mr. Hunt was headwaiter, he held a very formal position with respect and dignity. He wore a suit and tie to work every day, and he supervised the waiters, about twelve at any given time.

In fact, the elimination of waiters and waitresses at meals is of particular interest in its correlation to the retirement and death of Mr. Hunt. It was during the 1955–1956 school year—shortly after he retired, and right before he died in 1954—that waiters were no longer hired for the breakfasts and on weekends.[2] So by the time his children and grandchildren began their tenure of employment at the college, the world and even Hollins College had changed. Most colleges and universities had long before switched to cafeteria-style dining. None were serving students with waiters dressed in a formal style anymore. So Mr. Hunt's heirs had no opportunity besides being food-service employees earning minimum-wage salaries. Many of them had to take on additional jobs in Roanoke to keep from being destitute. The college offered them none of the educational opportunities or benefits that it offered to all of the other employees.

"I have to be somewhere else in a little while. You can just take the box," Ms. Hunt said.

"I am sorry. I didn't mean to keep you," I said.

"Come over and have a cup of coffee with me," Mrs. Bruce offered.

Back at Mrs. Bruce's house, I was finally able to relax. I flopped down in a big sofa chair by the window in the living room. African violets of pinks and purples bloomed everywhere. On the table to the right of me was her good wig that she had set in curlers so it would be ready for church on Sunday. Photographs of her grandchildren, great-grandchildren, and others graced the top of her brown piano. On one wall near another photograph of her grandchildren is her certificate for winning Hollins College's Algernon Sydney Sullivan Award. Mrs. Bruce is the first African American to have received the award, and probably the first staff person. She received it in 1976, the year she retired. The award states, "He reached out both hands in constant helpfulness to his fellow man." The award usually goes to a professor or benevolent alumna.

I didn't want to open the box from Ms. Hunt until Mrs. Bruce returned. She fussed around in her kitchen for coffee and a "little something to nibble on." As with my grandmother, I wasn't allowed anywhere near her kitchen.

She appeared with coffee and sweet potato pie. The pie melted in my mouth.

"I am so happy to be here," I said.

"It's sad isn't it? Our young people have no interest in their history."

"Why do you think that is?"

"They just don't understand how hard we've all worked and what we had to put up with."

"I guess I see it all the time with my students, too. All they seem to want to do is shop."

"That's sho 'nuff the truth. Child, I remember when we were coming up we used to go down to the college to shop. We didn't know what it was to go to Roanoke to buy clothes. The girls sold their clothes to us to get extra money. Someone would just say, 'I want a dress for Emma' or whoever. The next thing you know, you'll have it. The first pair of I. Miller shoes I wore were from there. A cousin called me and said, 'I got a pair of shoes for you.' I went over to see them. When I got those blue suede shoes, you couldn't tell me nothing," Mrs. Bruce laughed.

"I bet they were pretty."

"They were beautiful. To think those girls used to sell some of the prettiest clothes. We used to love to see the girls come after summer. We bought coats. My mama said, 'I want a coat for Sister' or Emma. I'd go over to the college to try it on; nine times out of ten it fitted."

"What other kinds of things did you get from the students?"

"When school would close, we used to go down to help Sister, who worked on the halls of the dormitories. We would go through their trash and take out all of their paper, pencils, and ink and tear out all of the leaves that had been used. That paper would get us through the winter because Mama would take charge of it when we got home and gave it to us as she thought we needed it."

"What else did you find in their trash?"

"Sometimes we would get good shoes and just good things that they threw away. We all missed that when we had to go to Roanoke and shop at Catos, Phelps, and all of those kinds of stores."

"Do you remember when that was?"

"Not exactly, but I wasn't a grown woman. Want some more coffee?" Mrs. Bruce asked.

"No thank you. I probably have taken up too much of your time already."

"This is a real treat for me. Can't think of anything I'd rather be doing."

"Well, maybe just another small piece of sweet potato pie."

Another photograph of Mr. Hunt that I found in the old box was one that is familiar around the college. In it, Mr. Hunt is dressed in a tuxedo and is ringing a huge dinner triangle.

Dean of Servants   65

Lewis Hunt ringing
the triangle.
Hollins Archives.

Lewis Hunt, Dean of Servants, and relatives.
Photo from Zackery Hunt; in collection of the
author.

"I have seen this one before," I said to Mrs. Bruce.

"That's the Lewis that everyone remembers."

"Do you know anything about the instrument?"

"I don't know where it came from. But everyone just thought it was like a dinner bell or something. But Lewis could play all kinds of tunes on it. And today, the Roanoke chapter of the Hollins Alumnae Association is named in honor of that instrument—the Triangle Alumnae Association."

"Really?"

"And not only that—after he died, folks picked it up and thought they could play it. No one never could. It was funny, really. We would hear the instrument and just shake our heads. Finally they just gave up. I wonder where it is now."

"What do you know about Mr. Hunt?"

"Look," Mrs. Bruce pointed to the lapel of Mr. Hunt's jacket in the photograph. "No one never saw him without a fresh flower on his lapel is what I heard."

"Was he in charge of all the workers in the dining hall?"

Lewis Hunt and waiters on steps of Cocke Memorial Building, circa 1920.
Photo from Zackery Hunt; in collection of the author.

"Just the waiters. Lewis was known to be a little heavy handed but ran a tight ship, if you know what I mean."

The next photograph we found was like something right out of Hollywood. Mr. Hunt is positioned in the center, wearing a black tuxedo, and on each side of him six waiters are wearing white jackets. They all wear white gloves.

"Do you know the names of any of these men?"

"Not right offhand, but if you can leave it with me, I will go over it with Sister and some more folks. We probably can come up with at least a few names."

"That would be great."

"You know, there was a social club and a singing group that most of Lewis's men were part of. Maybe there will be a photo of that in the box."

"Did they sing at the church?"

"Yes, and at the college too, particularly for holidays and special occasions. You would see them serving in the dining hall one minute and singing on stage the next."

"Like a glee club?"

"Yes. Child, Lewis Hunt was considered the head colored man around here for years. He came along after Clem Bolden and Caesar Morton. He was the last of the old-timers. We used to hear a story, that once the college received a distinguished guest from Africa. A dignitary of some kind. And Lewis wouldn't wait on him."

"Why?"

"Because, like I said, he was the head colored man around these parts. And he only served white folks."

The last article I found was Lewis Hunt's obituary:

In Memoriam
Lewis Hunt—Faithful Friend
Lewis Hunt, head waiter in the dining hall at Hollins College for 47 years, died at age 69 on September 4, 1954, at his home at Hollins after a long illness. When he retired in 1950, he had worked at the College for 52 years.

Thousands of Hollins College faculty and students knew Lewis, and his ready recognition of alumnae who returned for visits was phenomenal. His dignity was unassailable, his loyalty unquestioning and his innate courtesy unfailing.

His first job at Hollins as a boy of 13 was to tend a herd of sheep which grazed on the campus. From this he progressed rapidly to the dignified post of head waiter. Hollins still uses the sound of the triangle to call students to meals and through the years Lewis sounded this important call.

Lewis and Rosalie Hunt. Photo from Zackery Hunt; in collection of the author.

This obituary was the first I had ever read with no mention of a person's family, or anything personal outside of work. To test my theory I began reading obituaries in the newspapers, not just the Roanoke Times and World News, *but everywhere I traveled, and any other newspaper that I came across at the library at university where I taught. I was also saddened by the fact that Mr. Hunt had spent his retirement years sick.*

From the September 6, 1954, Roanoke Times, I learned that Mr. Hunt was survived by his wife, Rosalie, four daughters, and five sons, fourteen grandchildren, and three great-grandchildren. I felt pleased that I could include his family in this book.

Lewis Hunt with Matty Cocke, first
woman president of Hollins College
(1901–1933) and daughter of
Charles Lewis Cocke; circa 1952.
Hollins Archives.

Lewis Hunt, in front of the
Cocke Memorial Building.
Hollins Archives. This is the
last photo taken of Mr. Hunt.

The photograph of Mr. Hunt in the obituary was the same familiar one that is
displayed around the college. It was in the college's archives. I remembered when
I first saw it in the science building. I thought how proud and dignified he
seemed, dressed in his suit and bow tie and white gloves, to be serving white folks.

But then I had to look at the narratives that lie beyond the photographs and
beneath the stereotypes. At Hollins College, a different slave system had oper-
ated. But as far as I was concerned, slavery was slavery. The church offered the
community a cohesion and also acted as a refuge, providing a source of pride and
strength. But even there, everyone knew his place. The college was, indeed, the
"big house," and Lewis Hunt was part of the system. But within that system, he
rose to the highest possible position for an African American man. He was the
manager who supervised all of the other workers in the dining hall, which during that time was a very respected place.

The Price of Change

> Everything will change. The only question is growing up or decaying.
> Nikki Giovanni

Once again, I found myself lost in thought about the direction of my project. What would I do with the information I had gathered? Would anyone else from the community ever talk to me? I believed the Hollins Community reflected the city of Roanoke in many ways. For example, there never seemed to have been a civil rights movement in the city. The Hollins Community could have continued to exist only in such a passive and conservative city that was rooted in the churches, it appeared to me. The young folks didn't seem to stay in the area because of a lack of employment opportunities, which left old folks to run the city of Roanoke.

My teaching at Virginia Tech was demanding and at times overwhelming. I did not see how I could teach four classes per semester with any kind of excellence. I also found the students to be racist and sexist. And their attitudes were supported by the chairperson of the department, I believed. For example, he encouraged students to appeal their low grades, when most of the time, had he taken the time to inquire about the student's actual performance, he would have known that students were often irresponsible about their course work. I wasted too much of my time writing three-to-five-page letters defending my grading of students who didn't come to class half of the time. Each semester never truly ended, for there was always unfinished business carried into the next one. This zapped energy from the new term before it could begin. I felt like a servant who was being punished for a crime I didn't commit. I was also frustrated because this was taking time away from my Hollins project and Mrs. Bruce.

And as usual money was tight, but I knew that if I could just hang in there, my son would be out of college in a couple of years and my finances would improve. By this time he was in his sophomore year and earning good grades.

I knew it was time to see Mrs. Bruce. But before I telephoned her, she called me.

"I've been thinking of about you," she said, almost giggling.

69

"Same here," I answered.

"Well, my granddaughter, Cynthia, will be here next week. I thought maybe you'd like to meet her."

"That's a wonderful idea. Thank you for thinking of me."

"It will be good for our book."

"Please ask Cynthia to call me as soon as she gets in."

"I sure will."

"How've you been feeling?"

"Fairly well. Just worried about George some."

"What's wrong?"

"He wants to drop out of college."

"Why?"

"He says he doesn't want to play football anymore."

"He can still go to college without playing football."

"That's what I tried to tell him."

"Would you like for me to talk to him?"

"I sure would appreciate it."

"Better yet, my son will be home in two weeks. We'll have George over. Marcus is closer to his age. He will probably have more impact."

"Praise God."

"Don't worry; it will work out."

The week of my spring break I spent two full days researching information about Hollins College.

During Reconstruction, the Roanoke Valley had proven more amenable to African American labor than had most of the South; industrialization would benefit the area's African American citizens even as those in other regions were shut out from its benefits. For the African American population of the city of Roanoke, the choice of Roanoke as the headquarters of the Norfolk and Western Railroad in 1832 would be the watershed event in the growth of their numbers, if not their economical progress. As Roanoke historian Clare White wrote:

The black population of Roanoke had increased with the coming of the railroads as black men came to get jobs either in the shops or on the trains. Most of their wives and daughters worked as domestics for white families. Black men of leadership quality migrated into the city, primarily to the pulpits of the black churches.[1]

But the employment structure of postbellum southern railroads did not offer opportunities as significant for black workers as it did before the Civil War. "After the Emancipation, blacks in the South were relegated to low level positions as porters and laborers, a process hastened by the discriminatory policies of the all-white railway brotherhoods."[2]

Still, the Norfolk and Western—followed by the brick and glass plants in Salem, Virginia, and the sanatorium in Catawba, Virginia—was the largest source of employment for black men in the Roanoke Valley within a few years of its establishment. But ironically, these advances did not seem to shake the labor system at Hollins College. Transportation, tradition, and settlement patterns precluded the extension of railroad opportunities to the Hollins workers. Deedie Kagey writes, "Blacks drifted about and then settled in the communities around these sources of work. . . . Generally, they lived close to their work, perhaps being able to walk, and several generations continued in the same occupations."[3]

Another reason why the railroad didn't shake the employment situation at Hollins College probably had to do with the 66 percent of the workers at the college being women. Their names weren't recorded, but the numbers were there. The railroad was an employer of men. And the railroad had its own worker settlement in the city of Roanoke, since so much railroad employment was based on family connections.[4] The workers at Hollins College probably chose to remain where they were rather than enter a closed market. A list of black railway associations in the 1930s do not contain any of the familiar family names from the Hollins Community.

But at the college another kind of change was in the air. If the college was going to increase its student body from 300 to 450, greater efficiency in the workforce would also be necessary. The transfer of the college to public ownership was the single most significant factor to ending the paternalistic relationships and simple hierarchy that had for so long characterized the college— a more important change than even the necessary economies of the Depression. The second important factor in the change of Hollins's character came as the early figures of the institution gradually died out through the first decades of the century.

But World War I had not affected the labor conditions of the many servants who remained at the college in spite of demographic upheavals prior to the Depression. From 1880 to 1930, the black population of Botetourt County had fallen from 31.4 percent to 14.3 percent, and of Virginia from 41.8 percent to

26.9 percent, as blacks, especially men, moved northward to seek industrial jobs. As such, unemployment rates in 1930 were much lower for black men and women in the South than in the North: For women 8.2 percent in the North and 3.7 percent in the South; for men, 14.3 percent and 4.1 percent respectively.[5]

The continued focus of industrial development in the city of Roanoke contributed to the lack of discernible change in the employment and educational opportunities for the citizens of the Hollins Community and other African Americans. But the first high school for Roanoke's black children, Lucy Addison High, opened in 1916. Forty-six years before, public education would have ended with the eighth grade for black students. Mrs. Bruce is a graduate of Lucy Addison High School. She rode the bus from the Hollins Community to Roanoke for two years and lived in Roanoke with relatives for two more years.

Deedie Kagey wrote: "Attendance rates of black students were still low and school-aged populations stagnant between 1920 and 1940, prompting the school district to halve the number of black elementary schools when county schools were consolidated in 1921."[6]

The Hollins Community apparently had a stable or growing population, even as the black population in both counties declined overall. In 1921 a school was established in the Hollins Community for students living in both Roanoke and Botetourt Counties. This reorganized the integrity of the settlement despite the county line through the middle of the community.

A few days later I arrived home from teaching at Virginia Tech, bone-tired. I wanted to crawl into my bed and sleep for a week. My telephone answering machine light blinked. The message was from Mrs. Bruce. I smiled. Hearing her voice always made me smile. I called her back immediately.

"Guess what?" she asked.

"What?"

"Didn't I tell you that others in the community would talk?"

"You sure did."

"Well, today I received a telephone call from Harry Smith, and he wanted me to give you his telephone number."

"Really?"

"I don't know if you've seen him in church. But for sure I bet you've noticed his house. It's just across from the church on the west side and it has a little church built on the outside of the house."

"Yes. I know the house. I always wondered why the church was there."

"Now you can find out. Here is his phone number."

The first time I called Mr. Harry Smith I didn't get an answer, but I called back later in the evening. He spoke with an almost rough disk-jockey voice. He invited me to his house the following Tuesday afternoon.

In the meantime I lunched with Cynthia, Mrs. Bruce's granddaughter. She is a lovely young woman, with her grandmother's grace, but her wide smile belongs only to herself. She expressed appreciation for the work I was trying to do, but she was mostly happy that her grandmother was active in something she cared about—Mrs. Bruce had always believed in history, particularly their history, as far back as Cynthia could remember. She also told me that the message that Mrs. Bruce had given to her and her brother George for a long time was: "Get out of Roanoke. You'll never get a decent job, particularly at Hollins College." The only work that would be available to them there would be service work. Even when she was approached about enrolling at Hollins College, she wanted nothing to do with it. She did not believe that it was a place that would ever welcome her or anyone from the community on any form of equal grounds.

The day I visited Mr. Harry Smith was the same day that Alex Haley, the author of Roots, *died from a heart attack in Seattle. A part of me wanted to cancel the appointment to talk and grieve with friends. He had been a close friend of Nikki Giovanni's. And the year before he had been a guest at Virginia Tech during our Black History Month celebration. Everyone felt close to Alex Haley because he was so accessible.*

But I didn't cancel my appointment with Mr. Smith. Alex Haley didn't write Roots *by canceling appointments.*

Mr. Smith's house was like most of the other ranch-styled houses in the community, but he had added rooms to his house. After I knocked on the side door, a tall, thin man with gray hair and the same color of eyeglasses opened the door.

"I didn't know which door to use."

"This is just fine. Come in, Miss Smith."

"Thank you. Are we relatives?"

His wide grin lit up his face. "I would like to think so," he said.

"Before I sit down, I have to tell you what the first rule is."

He looked at me puzzled. "What?"

"Since we are relatives, you're going to have to call me Ethel."

Mr. Smith laughed out loud, showing all of his teeth. "It's a deal."

"Thank you for allowing me into your house to talk."

"Well, I've been thinking about it for a long time now, and figured I had a story to tell."

"First, I need your permission to record our conversation. That's a much more efficient way to make sure I get everything you say."

"Sure, that's fine. But before we get started, can I offer you something to drink?"

"I've just had lunch, but thank you very much. Who lives here with you?"

"I live here alone, since my wife died a few years ago."

"I am sorry."

"Thank you. I appreciate that."

"Tell me about the church in your yard."

"Well, I built it myself. It took me more than six months."

"Why did you build the church?"

"That was what our old church looked like before this new one was built. The one that I grew up in as a boy. And you know, I just didn't want to forget it. Thought I better do something about it before it was too late."

And do something about it, he did. Harry Smith's replica of the 1905 church has become a landmark of sorts for people familiar with the area. He couldn't bear to see the church he had grown up with destroyed, so he salvaged materials, including interior paneling and tin roofing, from the demolished structure and built his own four-foot-high replica. The detail is astonishing; the roofing is the same color red as the original; he has made stained-glass windows out of cellophane; and he built miniature pews to fit in the sanctuary. There is also a chimney, a vestibule, a pastor's study in the back, and, of course, a bell tower above the doorway. Adding to the replica's authenticity is the effect of weathering—as Smith once said, "I like it this way, because that was the way it was, weather-beated."

In an unanticipated way, Smith has perhaps increased the church's membership in a sense; the miniature church has become such a landmark that people come from all over to see it. It is particularly popular at Christmas, when Smith decorates it with lights. Students from Hollins ride horses into the Hollins Community to see it, for their instructors have told them about the community and Smith's church.[7]

"What do you think of the new church?"

"Well, let's put it like this: I don't go to church near as much as I used to," he laughed.

"Did you have any help building your church?"

"No, my wife was living when I first started the project. In fact, she used to fuss at me because I made a mess in the living room." Mr. Smith laughed again. He crossed his long legs, and for the first time I noticed that he was wearing white shoes that looked like they had been shined with a biscuit. In fact, Mr. Smith was a spiffy dresser. He sported a shirt with grey, black, and yellow patterns and a pair of gray bell-bottom slacks.

"Another thing I do is ask folks to write down for me all of your relatives as far back as you remember. It doesn't have to be in any order. Tell me if they are from your mother's or your father's side."

"Miss Emma told me you were a teacher, and you gave assignments."

"That's right. And in that way, you'll have some time to think about it. Name everyone—children, grandchildren, cousins, aunts, uncles, grandparents. Write their full names or as much as you remember, whether they are dead or alive, and any other thing you can remember about them—where they lived, their age."

"I can handle that."

"Good! I will pick up the list in a few weeks. But I will telephone you first. Mr. Smith, did you ever work at Hollins College?"

"No ma'am; well, not exactly."

"Did other members of your family work there?"

"Everybody did as far back as I can remember."

"Why didn't you work there?"

"Well, you see, it's like this. It was in the early 1940s. I will never forget it. I was about twelve years old, and in training to be a waiter. It was hot in that kitchen. Always hot in there, whether it was winter or summer, but sho 'nuff hot in the summer."

"What did you do before that?"

"Running around the college and the community doing whatever anyone told me to do. Everybody always worked, whether you was a grown person or a child."

"Was anyone training you to be a waiter?"

"Yes ma'am, one of Mr. Lewis Hunt's men. They ran the dining room like clockwork."

"What kinds of things were you told in training?"

"First, to be polite and always say 'Yes ma'am' to the young women. But most importantly, never, by no means, should we touch them in any way."

"So what happened?"

"On my first and last day as a waiter, I spilled hot coffee in one of the young women's lap."

"What happened then?"

"I don't know. Everything caved in on me. I always remember that feeling. Never been so scared in all of my life."

"Did you apologize to the student?"

"I sure did. But everyone just stopped and looked at me. I ran out of that dining room and never went back."

"Where did you go?"

"I went home and hid under the bed for what seemed like the longest time."

"But you had to come from under the bed at some point."

"That evening when both Mama and Papa come home. I was forced to come out."

"What did they say?"

"To be right honest, Miss Smith, we were pretty scared. Kept waiting for something to happen. Someone from the college to come and kick us off of the place."

"Remember, it's Ethel. Did anyone come?"

"No, but we were all pretty scared."

"But you were just a youngster yourself."

"I realized that, but we didn't know what was going to happen to us."

"Did anything ever happen to your family because of the accident?"

"No ma'am. Not that I know of, anyhow."

"Did you ever go back to the college?"

"To this day, I never set foot on the place again. But you know, it saved me from a life of servitude, now that I think about it. I went to work for the railroad and never looked back. My life turned out so much better. I am retired with a real pension."

"Congratulations! You certainly deserve it."

"Thank you so much."

"What are you going to do with your time now that you are retiring?"

"Travel, visit my children and friends. Always loved traveling since I worked on the railroad. I reckon it's in my blood."

Miniature First Baptist Church Hollins, built by Harry Smith. This photo was taken in 1995; the church no longer stands, due to weathering. Photo by Opal Moore.

A few weeks later I presented a lecture for the Roanoke Historical Society. I invited Mrs. Bruce, Mr. Smith, and anyone else in the community who wished to join me. To my delight, in addition to Mrs. Bruce and Mr. Smith, three other members of the community accepted my invitation. We arranged a time for me to pick them up. They all wore their Sunday best clothes. It was a proud day for all of us.

I introduced the members of the community to the audience. Without planning to when I introduced Mr. Smith, I told the story of his single day of employment in the Hollins dining hall. It was the first time I had repeated it, and I apologized to him for doing so. He nodded his head forward toward me, and I knew that it was all right.

A woman from the audience raised her hand, stood up, and said, "Harry, I am Shirley Henn. I was the one you spilled coffee on."

The audience clapped. And right before our eyes, something happened—we witnessed the process of healing.

"I am truly sorry," Mr. Smith said.

"I have always known that you were. It was just an accident. I don't know why it was such a big deal."

"Thank you for saying that."

"I have wanted to say that to you for about fifty years."

When Mr. Smith and Ms. Henn met each other halfway across the room and embraced, we all knew that that moment would be etched in our minds and hearts for a long time. The people in the audience were on their feet. Some of the women were wiping their eyes. We were all given gifts that afternoon.

Harry Smith, April 1999. Photo in
collection of the author.

The following poem was written for Mr. Smith by Katherine Soniat, a visiting professor at Hollins whose class visited and wrote about Mr. Smith's church.

Like Stars in a Dark Country Night

I see one bumblebee heading
over the fence and into the dollhouse
doorway of Old Fields Baptist Church.
The trees are tagged with signs
of modern advancement: KEEP OUT,
BAD DOGS, as out of the big house comes
a white-haired man saying
he's Harry Smith, maker of this
miniature church and everything
is copacetic if I want to take
a look. Just be sure to keep
him in my story.

The real church has vanished from
the hill but here's a little something

that'll keep—this six-foot long
god-house that Harry Smith built and kept
for months in his living room
before turning it out to winter.
I stoop for the peepshow—
four-inch pews scatter
like chance in the sanctuary;
wasps fly in novice formation,
wafer-thin wings, an offering;
six slender windows, cellophaned,
cast the nave in dusky, underwater blue,

and as I stand, I'm as tall
as the steeple strung with Christmas
lights, soaring in Wonderland
proportions over the tin roof's
peeling red coat.

No parishioners puzzle
in a stain of blue sunlight.
This church is cleansed
of people, of all but the ceremony
of cutting, the ritual of nailing
disappearance into place.

That night the big church came down,
it must have spread its cloistered parts
like stars in a dark country night
till Harry took charge and planted
in his yard what anyone will remember
of Old Fields Baptist Church.

Now I'm down on my knees again
peeking, and he's still saying
remember me. So, in the language
of installation, I commit Harry
and his church, hatched in a house,
to shine as blue as bedside stars
over Old Fields. Far away, a clock
chimes one hour before noon.
Harry's holding out his photograph
of the first, the big and the real
one. Somewhere it's midsummer.
Still mid-day.

7

The Voice of Mrs. Mary Emma Bruce, Historian and Philosopher

> And we be bringing, each of us
> the music of our selves to wrap
> the other in
>
> Forgiving clarities
> soft as a choir's last
> lingering note our
> personal blend
> I will bring you someone whole
> and you will bring me someone whole
> and we be twice as sure
> and we be twice as sure
> and we will have us twice as much
> of love .
> and everything.
>
> Mari Evans

I thought I would remember the spring of 1992 because it marked my fortieth birthday. But instead, I, along with most of the world, remember Rodney King's crying voice raising the question, "Can't we all just get along?" We watched the videotaped recording of Rodney King being beaten inhumanely by Los Angeles policemen. This incident, fused by other racial unrest, was the beginning of rioting and burning in cities all over America.

I was particularly concerned; my son was spending the second term of his junior year of college at Morehouse College, in Atlanta, Georgia, one of the cities where rioting was happening. I wasn't scared because he was with family, and we spoke every day on the telephone. But I was alarmed when friends telephoned me to express their concern. My son and I survived that awful week. But it was an awakening for both of us, particularly for him, regarding how volatile race relations are in America. Something positive happened between us; the L.A. Riots, as they came to be known, had prompted my son and me to discuss openly the conditions of race in this country.

By then I had known Mrs. Bruce for more than two years. I knew her schedule and was generally able to track her down. She also knew which days I taught *at Virginia Tech and my tennis schedule. We both liked it that I didn't call for appointments anymore. In contrast to our initial formality, I just dropped in on her, like folks do at home. And I had long ago given up the notion of stopping in just for a few minutes. I had learned to just let her talk—and not ask too many questions, just enough to get her started.*

This interview was taped on my front porch at 403 King George Avenue Southwest, in Roanoke, Virginia, in the early spring of 1992. I had just planted pansies in the huge urns on the steps and hung Boston ferns from the ceiling of my front porch. I thought Mrs. Bruce would enjoy the scenery. She had never seen where I lived. From my front porch the steel star on top of the mountain, representing Roanoke as a progressive "star city," could be easily seen.

My interview began with a simple question. "Where did you grow up?"

"Right in Hollins, Virginia. I lived in Roanoke for two years with Ruth Hughes to finish up school there. A girlfriend and I used to ride the bus to school every morning. Then something happened that the little bus was cut off. I don't remember what. And we stayed in Roanoke, and I stayed with Ruth Hughes and finished at Addison High School."

"Tell me about your family."

"Mama stayed at home to take care of us. Of course, she took in laundry from the college. Child, I can still pick up six pounds of irons. No one thought that I could. I kept the irons that Mama used to iron the girls' clothes from Hollins. They're somewhere in my house. We children helped out around the house as much as we could. Everyone always worked. We washed in the big barrels that caught the rainwater, or the creek water that Papa would tote to the house. It was eight of us children in all. Now only my sister Alice and I are left. Papa worked at Rockydale Quarry. I think we sometimes got along better in those days than folks do today."

"Did you go to the little school down on the corner of the community? The little wooden one that was turned into a store?"

"No. no. no. That was built for a store. That's never been a school. The lady that lives there, her mother and them owned that store. They built it. The school where I went to was right up there where that water tower is; our school was right in that spot."

"Who was your teacher at that school?"

"His name was Samuel Carrington and he used to walk up from Cloverdale up the hill to teach school."

"Was he the only teacher?"

"He was the only teacher, and he walked up the hill every morning. He

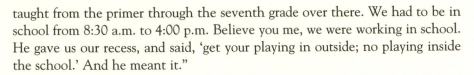

taught from the primer through the seventh grade over there. We had to be in school from 8:30 a.m. to 4:00 p.m. Believe you me, we were working in school. He gave us our recess, and said, 'get your playing in outside; no playing inside the school.' And he meant it."

"Is that school closed now?"

"Yes, it's torn down. All of those old schools are torn down now. Three of us had bought that building when the school was going to be sold and we said we wanted the community to have it. Three of us—Ruth Hughes, John Francis, and myself—we bought it. Got it for fifteen hundred dollars. We were going to give it to the community. One statement was made by Mr. Francis that throwed it. When he said, 'I would be glad to give it over to them, but I would like to see them use it for the purpose we bought it for. And that was to have recreation for the old people coming on. We don't want nothing with strings tied to it.' I couldn't see where there were strings tied. So the school is gone. We just don't have a place for children to have recreation, to have their parties. Maybe that school would have been the ideal place; had water and everything there. You take that Sweet Shop there, which belongs to my niece. It would be a nice thing if she would consider selling it. You know, right on the corner. You'll see that big brick building standing there and it says 'The Sweet Shop' with poison ivy growing up on it. I said to her, 'Why don't you let us take that and open it up and have a family business there?' But she never seemed to want to do that. I told her it's going to fall in and everything. It's too nice of a building to just let it fall down. I don't see why she wouldn't want to do that. When her husband was living, they ran the place, but now to get a hot dog you have to go all the way up to Hollins. Nothing but Ash Bottom here. You go out that road, and you can't get up in Ash Bottom. The school bus goes up there and turns around."

"What is Ash Bottom?"

"That's a section of the community that was given that name because a lot of ash trees growing up there. They just called it Ash Bottom because it's kind of lowland up there. There used to be quite a few houses up there. My uncle used to live at the far end of that road after you get up there and we could cut across the mountain. This is little Tinker [Mountain] here but goes on the other side of and goes across and comes down through the 'old field.' There used to be a lot of farmland up there, but they put it to rest and called it 'old field.' "

"Is that where the first slaves who worked at Hollins College lived in the beginning?"

"When the slaves first came here they lived at the college. They used to have little houses down there. You know where the horse stables are; down the hill from there, there was about three or four houses. That's where they first lived.

Some of those slaves lived on campus with the girls to take care of them. That's what I was told. But when they started raising their families they needed somewhere to put their children. Mr. Cobb gave some to the slaves, a portion of the land out there to build them little houses. We've been trying to figure out how much. It must have been on that side joining the college property, because all of this, over this way, came from Mr. Reed. He had had the largest portion of land that was recorded in Salem [Virginia]. So now the college got all of that land back, as far as I know."

"Isn't the walk from the community to the college much closer than where the stables are?"

"Much closer. It was even further because, you see, the stables haven't always been up on that hill. Plus the houses were further back toward the creek. Folks used to call them people 'people living up on the creek,' is what I was always told. But folks used to walk further than that. My brother worked in Fincastle and walked every day. I know that's more than ten miles. He just walked over the dam to work. You cross Interstate 81 at the intersection; he walked across that. There were a lot of men who went over there and cleaned up that place. There used to be a settlement up there. But the men from here went over there when they weren't working at the college and tore those houses down and helped to clean them out. I will tell you another thing: There was no way to ride. Folks didn't have cars and such like today."

"Did you walk to work?"

"Yes, I walked across the field to work. I walked every morning."

"Does the path still exist?"

"We called that part of the community Rocky Branch; the road is there, at least part of it. Where that big water tower is, well that road comes up that far, but the rest of Rocky Branch is growed up. As far as I know there is but one house down there now that's really Rocky Branch."

"Do you know what is left of the path?"

"Well they just made a road out there. You know how you go and just make a road anywhere. They just made a road across there. The horses and wagons would go across that way and people would walk that way."

"Why is the path called Rocky Branch?"

"Because there's a branch that goes across there. And rocks were placed there for small children, or anybody, but particularly small children, to have a path to the college without going on the main highway. Water runs under those rocks. Would you believe I played under the dam? I was supervising Miss Lithornia Gibbs when she came here to Hollins as a community leader. She organized a Girl Reserve group instead of Girl Scouts. We would hike across the field up there to what we called then was the falls. The dam where it is now was known as the falls, and we used to go up there and that water would be falling over the rocks. We played under them many, many days. It was settled up there then. Then after they cleared out the dam is right where the fall used to be. We used to go over there and have our little picnics up there and play in the water and come back down across the field.

"I forgot to mention that in the beginning, when I was telling you about our little school, this lady came here from North Carolina. She was Miss Lithornia McFarland when she came to Hollins. She was our community leader, and she had organized us into groups, by age, I would say. Then Miss McFarland and Reverend L. K. Jackson got together with some of the people at the college because they wanted to consolidate the schools. We had a little white school up there where the water tower is now. And another one in 'Oldfield,' and a little school over there that was the county school. That was Botetourt County over here, and they wanted to consolidate the schools, so each county had to raise twenty-five hundred dollars to help, and we did. So Miss Gibbs said to us, 'you children are going to the schools and you are going to work for and help make the twenty-five hundred dollars.' It looked to me like every day we were going somewhere with a play, wrapping May poles, and beating drums. Every week we had to raise this money to consolidate the schools. We used to go to the college with our plays. About the second week in May, they'd always give us a program at the college for our church. Miss Gibbs and Mr. McFarland married. And they would take us children down to the college every Christmas.

"It's like I don't understand all this confusion about integration. We didn't know anything about being integrated. All of us—I forget what they used to call the white folks who lived down by the creek, but the white people lived down here on the road, and all of those children and all of these children in the community—we used to go down to the college together for Christmas treats. The same day and in the same place. We played together. We never knew all of the commotion like they're having now about integration. They used to play ball here. Those white children used to come over here and play. We all just played together. We just didn't have problems. I just don't understand why we have to have it today, because we never had it before. We all had to live and work together, even went to church together sometimes. A little while back I was invited to a luncheon for the folks in the community at the college to celebrate Black History Month. I found all of the black folks sitting at one table, and the whites at another. That's just not the way it used to be. Hollins was better than that.

"We also used to work for Charlie Nininger's [a local merchant] then some on the weekends after we finished up at Hollins. We'd get up on Saturday mornings and carry those clothes down there and we come back with all the vegetables we could carry. They probably didn't give us a dollar for washing and ironing the laundry, but we could get all the food we could carry. That was quite a ways to walk, too."

"Where was the house you were born in?"

"You know that big white house where the bushes have been pushed up? Me and Mama had a little three-room house right in the back of that. There was about six of us that were living in that little house right behind that big one. Then my papa built a house up there on the hill. That must have been back in 1918 when he built the house up here, and that's where we all grew up.

"That was before his accident at the quarry. That's when I first got it in my head that I wanted to be a nurse. I changed the bandages on his crushed legs and took his temperature. It made me feel so good to take care of him."

"What about rain or other bad weather? Did you still work on the weekends?"

"We'd put on our raincoats and boots and go ahead. When it rained, snowed, hailed, or whatever, I'd do the same thing and go to the college. Mrs. Robert Stewart, who taught in the chemistry department, went home one Christmas and she brought me a fur coat back. She said it belonged to her aunt. The coat was too heavy for me. She said it was for me to walk in. I could not carry that coat. Therefore, I went to wearing two and sometimes three sweaters under my coat. Then I'd put on my boots. We never had no such thing as a snow day or any other day off due to bad weather. If you had a job, you got down there the best way you could. That's the way it was."

"How old were you when you first worked at the college?"

"My gracious, I went to the little brick school. And when I finished the seventh grade here in Hollins, I went to Lucy Addison High School for six years. Of course, I loved science and I took all of the maths that they taught in high school. And then when I came out of high school, I was asked to come to Hollins College to work with one of the elder maids. We all called her Aunt Bill Hunt. I worked with Aunt Bill for one year. Then I went to Roanoke and worked for Dr. A. Willis Robinson.

"When I left there, the head of the chemistry department wanted somebody to work with her. Mrs. Harriet Fillinger, head of the chemistry department, asked for me because I had worked in her building, and she knew I was the maid with Aunt Bill. She asked for me to come. Several went down, but she wouldn't accept none but Emma! So 'Emma' went to work in the chemistry department in 1934. I worked there under Miss Fillinger for about two years before she turned me loose in the department. We talked about school for me; I told her I wanted to major in chemistry, but Papa had had an accident and there was no money for me to go to college. Soon after that, I started to study freshman chemistry with Professor Fillinger. I learned which chemicals caused which reactions, and I memorized the periodic table of elements. I sometimes took the tests along with the students. I made all A's!

At the end of two years, I was in charge of all of the chemicals in the department. I gave out all of the chemicals. I prepared all the experiments for the freshman class. Doing that, I had to make up all of the solutions, test all of it before it was put in the lab for the girls to use. In the meantime, I only worked there from one to four p.m.

"Miss Sitler asked me to come to work in the biology department; another part of the science that I loved was biology. I would go there from four to six p.m. In the biology department, I took care of the little animals and helped the girls prepare those little animals. You know when they mount those birds and killed the snakes, drowned the snakes, whatever way they do it, I was there to help them to do that. I helped in the mounting of these things. We had a big order that we used to put these things in. But in the chemistry department I was in charge of all chemicals, explosives, and what-have-you. Never had an accident while I was there. I worked there until 1976 when I retired from the chemistry department. From then on I began to work for different ones of the faculty in their homes like I still do. I am now eighty-two years old."

"Why did you leave the chemistry department?"

"Well, I was sixty-five. But they did ask me if I would consider staying on for another year. I didn't do that. I felt like I was tired of it, and Miss Fillinger had passed on. The ones that were living when I started to work there had passed on. When young people come in every year, somebody new and something different, so I said, 'Emma's getting old and she better get on out from here while the going is good.' So I retired."

"They must have been lost when you left."

"Well, they said they were lost and asked me to come back and work, but I didn't go back. I was established with my other friends and I was enjoying what I was doing. I still enjoy my work because every day I see somebody new. I don't have to be bothered with the same person every day. It's a new one every day and I enjoy that. Some folks say I ought to give up work, but I don't see no reason to.

"I haven't been in the labs since they changed them. When I started in the chemistry department it was in Pleasants Hall. In taking care of those chemicals in the summer I had to bring down the bottles of all explosives and put it in the locked box on the outside for safety. Then I had to climb about three flights of steps in going back and forth to do this or that. I had to carry the other chemicals that were not explosive to the attic for safety.

"But the best part is that in the old building, I had a flower garden on the landing onto the attic and we used to raise tomatoes up there. In April we had tomatoes on our vines in the old building. I grew all kinds of African violets in the old building. That's when I first started growing African violets—and have been growing them ever since. Let's see; I don't know anything else to tell you. I didn't do no physics."

"How much money did you earn?"

"Let's see; what did I get in 1934? I know I did some extra work, and Miss Moore gave me fifteen cents an hour for that. Back in 1934 they paid me six dollars a week when I first went there to work in the afternoon from one to four p.m. Each year they would give just a little raise, but I was basically getting six dollars a week."

"Five days a week?"

"Yes, and I worked on Saturday mornings, too. With the six dollars a week, I was also getting my meals. I could go down there and eat three meals a day. I would go for breakfast and lunch, but there wasn't no point for me to go back for supper when I was already at home. That was back in the 1930s. I don't think anybody else was getting much more than that. I guess I worked down there for about fifteen years or more before they put me on a regular payroll. That's when my salary went up."

"Were you paying into Social Security?"

"Not the fifteen years that I was making six dollars a week. They weren't taking anything out."

"Why do you think there was no pension plan?"

"Well, if you weren't on the regular payroll that probably had something to do with why there was no pension plan. And then as the laws got tighter, they were forced to follow them."

"Do you know anyone in the community who has a pension?"

"I doubt it seriously whether there is anybody now getting a pension from the college."

"Do you receive any retirement benefits?"

"Not from Hollins College."

"What about the children of the members of the community? Were they able to attend the college and receive the same benefits as the children of the other employees?"

"The faculty children can go for free. It hasn't been that long since they made that offer to the community, so I have been told. I tried to get Cynthia to look into it. But she wouldn't. But I will tell you one thing, though, there was a [black] woman from Roanoke who used to work over there in one of the offices. There was a secretarial job coming up, and she put it an application, but they wouldn't hire her for that. They simply wouldn't give it to her. She never did say why, but she didn't get that job."

"Why did you think she didn't get the job?"

"I can't rightly say, since I don't know her skills, but I surely have some ideas."

"What are your ideas?"

"I only speak what I know!" Mrs. Bruce laughed.

"Does the community have a close relationship with the college today?"

"Not like we used to. They don't come to our church like they used to; there was a time when we could always depend on those students in our church. But now, I guess since they have their own cars and can go into Roanoke or else-where. But we used to always have a crowd of girls from the college over here."

"What about the faculty members?"

"Yes. And them too, especially if someone died or got married. We knew that we could count on the college to be there."

"When did you notice things changing?"

"Well, let me see, since I haven't worked over there since 1976, I can only speak about the church. It seems to me like when the Civil Rights Movement came, the college dropped us like a hot potato. It was an opportunity for them not to take even the little responsibility that they used to take. And, of course, new teachers and staff made a difference as well. They didn't know us like the older ones did. So as the older ones retired and died out, we got left behind again."

"Let me know if you're tired—"

"Child, I am enjoying myself too much, but I'd like to just sit a while. It's so peaceful. I am often so busy that I sometimes forget to just sit and listen to the world."

"But you are busy doing for everyone. Just think if more folks were like you the world would so much better off."

"Well, I do what I can."

Mrs. Bruce and I sat on my front porch and sipped lemon tea with fresh mint from my garden. We witnessed the late afternoon fading into early evening. There was really no need to talk as we listened to the end of the day—the city of Roanoke at the top of the hill and folks coming home from work. Early spring critters hummed in the yard. Even the blue jays sang.

There was so many questions I wanted to ask Mrs. Bruce, but didn't know how to raise. For example, I wanted to know more about her personal life. But like all southern ladies she owned her private life, and I understood about not crossing those lines. After all, she had given me so much with such graciousness.

Emma Bruce, after retirement from Hollins College, 1976. Collection of Mary Emma Bruce.

Her spoken words and the spirit of her voice created one of the strongest bonds I had ever experienced, apart from motherhood. I knew that I would forever be transformed because of her. She had lit a spiritual light for me that I hoped would never stop burning. Her voice was tied up with the creation of an authentic public and political voice that she didn't even realize. But what she did understand so well were her duties and responsibilities as a Christian and a citizen.

The Lord Keeps Me

Over my head
I see freedom in the air
Over my head, Oh Lord
I see freedom in the air
Over my head
I see freedom in the air
There must be a God
somewhere
                    Negro Gospel

I attended church services at Hollins First Baptist to celebrate the life and work of fifty-eight-year-old poet and essayist Audre Lorde. She had finally lost her fourteen-year battle against breast cancer. I knew her poetry well; it exhibits a strong sense of responsibility to the truth with the collective history and experiences of black women throughout the world.

I had listened to a program about her life from the National Public Radio station. Women, in particular, paid tribute to her. Eulogies to her were printed in many newspapers. But I didn't feel like talking to anyone. I cleaned my house, lit candles, and listened to the early music of Miles Davis, who had died the previous year.

Later in the semester I met a new professor at Hollins College: Marilyn Moriarty, a Shakespearean scholar and writer. I told her about my work with the community. Because of her generous support and knowledge in grant writing, I received a fellowship from the Virginia Center for Creative Arts for two weeks for that summer to work on my Hollins project. I received several other grants after that as well. The grant from VCCA was the first I had received other than the three hundred dollars from Hollins College. Two weeks of uninterrupted time to work on my research sounded like heaven to me. Mrs. Bruce, as always, was supportive and happy. She believed "that it was just a matter of time before our work could be done." She was also happy that her grandson, George, was now continuing his education at Virginia Tech, even though he was no longer playing football. And her granddaughter, Cythnia, was working on a master's degree. My son was back at Wesleyan University in Connecticut beginning his senior year. We had reasons to celebrate and be thankful.

The church has always been at the helm of African American communities whether the occasion is political, economic, social, or, of course, religious. The Hollins Community is no different. I often raised the question to myself: How can black folks be such dedicated Christians after being enslaved? Mrs. Bruce taught me that in God there was strength and the source for patience to wait for freedom. But she also believed that one had to work while waiting. That was a compromise I could live with.

Since Mrs. Bruce had served as church secretary for, as she put it, "more years than I can remember," I wanted to talk to her about her role in the church and the history of the congregation.

"Did you serve as an officer of the churches at any time?"

"No, I didn't. Not officially, anyway."

"What do you mean?"

"Well, for a long time I was the secretary—took down the minutes and did all of the correspondence for the church—because I was one of the only ones who could read and write. But since I am a woman, I wasn't allowed to be an official member of the board of directors."

"How did you feel about that?"

"I see it like this: I was working for the Lord. Didn't care nothing about some official title. Whatever work needs to be done, I do it if I can. Getting flowers, cleaning the church, cooking, working with the young people. There is plenty of work to keep us all busy. And since I was doing the work, and everyone knew I was doing the work, I was the church secretary. Child, the Lord keeps me."

She reminded me of Mrs. Willie Mae Ford, known as the mother of gospel music, who traveled the country singing and preaching in a vibrant, intense style, which was often in opposition to established church practices. "When I would go to their meetings, the preachers would say, 'You can sit down there, you don't need to come up here. Don't get in my program. You're a woman, didn't you realize?' No respect at all. Well, it don't make no difference to me. So I turn around in my pew and sing to that audience. Next thing I know, 'Come on up here, get up and let all of them see you.' See God don't want no filter on His work. To be a gospel singer, you got to be a gospel person."[1]

Another irrepressible female church leader is Dorothy Height, the president of the National Council of Negro Women since 1957. The organization was founded in 1935 by Mary McLeod Bethune. Height said, "Black women are the backbone of every institution, but sometimes they are not recognized as even being there, even in the Civil Rights Movement. There was a myth across the South, that the only two free people were the white male and black woman, and that black women had better chances at jobs. Well, that was because they scrubbed floors.”[2]

"Mrs. Bruce, tell me about the churches in the community."

"The first church was probably built around 1892, or even before that. It was called Lovely Zion, and it was built straight up from the ground. But as the community grew, they built another church in 1905, and that one stood until 1967 when we pushed it down over the hill—as we always called it, burying the church. The name was changed to First Baptist Church Hollins. We have a membership of about 300 people. We organized our missionary circle, which is about a hundred years old. It's going to celebrate its birthday on Sunday. We have had a number of ministers. Our first pastor was . . . Oh, it slips my mind at the moment, but I will think of it. Then we had Reverend Price and Reverend J. J. Jefferson, L. K. Jackson, E. T. Brown. All of those were great men who pastored and taught us. Then we had Reverend G. Thomas Turner, Reverend Braxton Brodie, Reverend J. A. Keaton, and our present pastor, Reverend Charles Calloway. Reverend E. G. Hall, who pastored us in the 1960s, was the man who built the brick church that we have now. We went into that church in 1967. After Reverend Keaton came, he built more to the church—the seven classrooms, a new kitchen, and then we put in two furnaces because the first one we had was the old section of the church, and we had one for the new section. We have air conditioning now in our church. It's quite a beautiful little church."

"I understand that you have quite some choirs in the church."

"We do. We have four choirs. I would love for you to hear our children sing. I know you've heard us old folks on Sundays. But our children are just great! They're in a musical seminar all this week. They're going to give a concert at the Roanoke Civic Center, Sunday at seven p.m. Advance tickets are three and five dollars at the door. Not just our children alone. We have about twenty-five to thirty of ours in this choir, what they call the Valley Baptist Choir. All in all, it's about 150 children in that choir."

"Where will the seminar be held?"

"The seminar will be held at High Street Baptist Church. The concert will be given at the Civic Center. The rector said on Sunday that twenty-three people had registered for this seminar. I know we sponsored one. My sister helped with one and we got them over there. We used to have a mass choir with the children, and once a year we'd go over to the college and sing. They called us the memorial choir."

"Tell me about the cemetery."

"It's been there since 1882. But before we started to be buried here, up the road where the ITT plant is, was a little church up there called the Green Ridge Baptist Church. Half of the people here went to Green Ridge, and the other half went over to what is known as Mount Moriah. If you lived in Roanoke County, you went to Green Ridge, and if you lived in Boutetourt, you went to Mount Moriah. Quite a few of our folks were buried in Green Ridge. You can see one tomb up there in Green Ridge yard, just one. But there's quite a few graves that was there. They have cleaned the cemetery out now.

"During the time when we went to church in Green Ridge, we used to still have a little church here when I was coming up, but we went to Green Ridge because it was still in action. Before we got our real church, there were some ladies that used to do the cleaning on the halls. They used to wait [serve] in the dining halls. They used to go up to Green Ridge on Sunday mornings for Sunday school, and they would leave before the service was over and come back to serve dinner [lunch] in the dining room at the college. The lady who told me this, her name was Rosa Bolden, and she told me a number of them used to go up there and they had to run many a morning from Green Ridge to Hollins College. See, at that time it [the highway] wasn't built up. They had a straight shot from across the creek and [could] be right at the college. Then the people living out in the community used to do the laundry for the girls."

"Does anyone know who's buried up there?"

"Not now. They don't because all of the tombs are gone. It's just a clean field now. Just that one grave. You'll see that grave that was right in front of the church under a tree. The tree is not there now, nothing but that tomb."

"Whose one grave is it? Does anybody know?"

"Let's see, what is that lady's name? I know who it is, but I can't think of her name right now. She was a Godfrey. It wasn't Miss Nancy Godfrey, because she was buried at Green Ridge, but that was her daughter who was buried in front of the church."

"Is Mount Moriah still there?"

"That church is still in action."

"What about their cemetery?"

"The cemetery is still there. When they built the church here, we began to use the cemetery over at Mount Moriah to bury people."

A few days later I decided to search for Mount Moriah Church. Within minutes after I turned off of the busy Roanoke highway of Orange Avenue, I knew I had stepped into another world. I walked up the hill to the church. I had telephoned Mrs. Louise Witt, one of the twelve members of the church. She seemed very pleased that I was interested in the history of her church, as she showed me around proudly.

After my visit to Mount Moriah, I was so excited. Other folks had to know about this church. I stopped by my friend Anna Lawson's house. We talked for a long time about history and race relations in the South. She was working on her dissertation on the history of the African Americans in Williamsburg, Virginia. Later I visited another friend, Mary Bishop. She had never heard of Mount Moriah, but she shared my enthusiasm.

The following week Mary Bishop and I returned to the church. Our visit inspired her to compose the following article.

Call to Worship

It is not Roanoke's grandest tabernacle, but little Mount Moriah Baptist Church is one of city's oldest. All that its few remaining members desire now is indoor plumbing--and a chance to grow.

High above the fast food and the fast trucks, up a tree-lined lane off busy U.S. 460 on Roanoke's eastern fringe, sits a simple white clapboard church. Step inside and you are in the sanctuary of your grandparents: Long-handled wicker collection baskets. Funeral-home fans. Oil lamp chandeliers. Wooden flower stands handmade by deacons of decades ago.

A coal fire in a pot-bellied stove heats the cinder-block fellowship hall. Tiny Bibles from the 1870s lean against each other on the shelves. Huge hand-sewn stitches in thick thread hold a cloth cover on an old hymn book. "Just think," says church member Louise Witt, gently holding the hymnal and gazing at the stitches zigzagging across its back. "Our ancestors did that."

Mount Moriah Baptist Church has endured from the days of slavery. Slaves of 19th-century Hollins College President Charles Lewis Cocke reportedly started the church in 1858. Stories passed down say that even though it was illegal to teach slaves to read, Cocke hid slaves in a covered wagon and whisked them to nighttime reading lessons and Bible school.

A dozen devoted church members, some descendants of those slaves, still come to fourth-Sunday services in the sanctuary, which is more than a century old itself. It is the third building in the congregation's history. They carefully dust the rough-hewn wooden tables, benches and coat racks made by their ancestors. Louise and Silas Witt, a couple in their 60s, haul lawn mowers from home to carefully trim the expansive church yard and nearby cemetery.

Faithfully every spring and fall, members scrub the kitchen stove and fridge. They launder and iron the curtains. "We just keep it up like we do our homes," Louise Witt said. "This is our home." More than anything, members want at long last to have indoor plumbing and a bathroom for their congregation, one of the oldest in the Roanoke Valley.

Then, maybe their church could grow again. The dishes could be scoured after lunch in the fellowship hall. Their elderly friends wouldn't have to trudge in their Sunday finest across the church's backyard to an outhouse. "You can't grow if you don't have water," said the Reverend Thomas E. Pleasant, acting pastor.

Mount Moriah began as a "brush arbor," a thatched-roof, open-air shelter that slaves fashioned, African-style, from the logs and branches of the surrounding woodlands. Oral history has it that they began meeting somewhere near the current church site, perhaps where Charles Cocke took them for reading lessons. . . .

In her 1988 book, *When Past Is Prologue: A History of Roanoke County*, Deedie Kagey wrote that court records show a Charles L. Cocke owning 18 slaves during the Civil War. Roanoke County's "slave schedule" for 1860 lists a Charles Cocke owning two male slaves. Though Cocke apparently was a slaveholder, Alvord Beardslee, professor of religion at Hollins, says, "Cocke's papers show his disdain for the institution of slavery. Cocke once wrote that Africans should never have been enslaved and forced to come to this country." . . .

Church members regard Cocke as a forefather. "They used to talk about him and say he was a wonderful man," Louise Witt said. "He had to have been nice to his slaves to teach them to read and write."

Five years after beginning services in the brush arbor, Mount Moriah's members built a small, enclosed building of wooden slabs. It also had an African look, a thatched roof. It was called the African Baptist Church. Then, perhaps because it's on a hill, it became Mount Moriah, probably named after the Jerusalem mountain mentioned in II Chronicles 3:1. The current sanctuary was built about 1873 and the fellowship hall in the early 1950s. For the congregation's 100th anniversary in 1958, members installed a furnace and electric lights.

Sitting on a knoll surrounded by woods, Mount Moriah is hallowed ground to members. "It's my roots, my family. My grandfather pastored here," says Louise Curtis Thompson, clerk of the church more than 30 years. Members believe slaves may be buried in unmarked graves in the cemetery. The people of Mount Moriah feel the weight of African American history in their church. They are determined to save it.

"Till this building falls down," Louise Witt says, "we'll be right here." For months, she's been writing City Hall and state and local agencies, trying to get a plumbing grant. She's been turned down every time. Money's available for homes, not churches.

Families pledge all the money they can to Mount Moriah, but when there are only 12 members, it's hard to drum up the thousands of dollars— maybe $10,000—to get water to the building and then to build a bathroom. Just last year, members paid $500 for a new roof. Pastor Pleasant hopes a bigger church or some religious organization will help them get plumbing. He's certain that the faithfulness and prayers of his members will bear fruit. "If we don't get it one way," he said cheerfully, "we'll get it another."

It's amazing Mount Moriah has survived. There have been attempts to buy its property, once for a shopping center, once for a trucking company. U.S. 460 nibbled a bit of land when the road was widened years ago. The Vinton Historical Society met there not long ago. "A lot didn't even know the church was here," said Louise Witt. You can't see the church from the highway.

At one time it was a thriving congregation with 60 or more members and seminary-trained ministers. Members lived in log cabins and other homes near the church.

The eldest member, 82-year-old Dollie English, has belonged since she was 10. "When I first started coming here, I came in a horse and buggy," she said. She recalled big homecomings at the church every fourth Sunday in July.

Lay members have kept the church going. One Sunday in September, members honored their last pastor, the Reverend Willie A. Andrews, a retired composing-room custodian at the *Roanoke Times & World-News*. He had a stroke and is in a wheelchair. His children and grandchildren wheeled him out onto his front porch on Orange Avenue, Northwest. Seven Mount Moriah members surrounded him and reverently settled a plaque into his lap. It called him "a good and faithful servant" of the Lord. "That's so nice," he said.

Pleasant, a retired General Electric worker, has been pastor since Andrews became ill three years ago. As elderly members die one by one, those remaining fear that the church will perish, too, but they and Pleasant won't give up. "He really held us together," Louise Thompson, 69, said. She's been a member since she was 12. Some of her family moved on to bigger churches, the ones with central air conditioning and Sunday school rooms. But she decided not to go. "No," she said, "I am staying."

Her grandfather, the Rev. Thomas C. Curtis, is buried in the church cemetery. Born in 1857, he was pastor of the church from 1901 until his death in 1933. "I have fought a good fight," says his gravestone, quoting II Timothy 4:7. "I have finished my course, I have kept the faith."

The congregation has set up a fund to get water and plumbing in the church. Contributions may be sent to Mount Moriah Baptist Church Improvement Project, P.O. Box 181, Vinton, VA 24179.[3]

I reread Deedie Kagey's book and thought about what she stated about Charles Lewis Cocke with regard to the education of members of the Hollins Community: "Peonage and sharecropping were the agricultural South's solution to regaining authority over black labor after emancipation. Stability at Hollins College was helped also by the Antebellum education of blacks and C. L. Cocke's role in providing it."

According to Kagey, "Cocke was furthermore instrumental in the founding of Enon Baptist Church, which received blacks as members through the War and was the only church in the Roanoke area which is known to have received and instructed blacks." Kagey's history states that Cocke established Sunday school classes for Enon's black members after 1855, though he was not the instructor: In the summer of 1855 the church began Sunday school classes for the black slaves and servants of Cocke. They were received into church membership, but their instruction continued under separate supervision by persons considered suitable.[4]

From the Minutes of the 1866 Valley Baptist Association of Virginia

The report was read by C. L. Cocke, as follows:[5]

Your committee on the Religious Instruction of the Colored people would respectfully submit the following report:

The action of the Federal Government in violently severing the relations which formerly subsisted between the white and colored races of our State, has placed the latter, for the present at least, in a more dependent condition than they were when in a state of domestic slavery. In their former condition they had homes, food, clothing, and medical attention when sick, but now they are destitute of all such comforts, except so far as their wants are supplied by the white race. Formerly they had regular employment and intelligent human guardians to direct their labors and to defend them from imposition and violence; now no parties stand forth as their peculiar friends and protectors, but they have been cast out upon a cold and unfriendly world, with all the prejudices of race an color against them, unprepared by previous training to meet the responsibilities of life, or successfully contend with those obligations and exactions which society everywhere imposes upon its members. Destitute of means, of education, of moral training, and, as a race, notoriously improvident and defective in wise foresight, their condition is one which appeals to us in the strongest terms for sympathy and counsel.

That they shall ever rise to positions of social equality and commingle with the white race in all the relations and avocation of life, the indications of Providence, if not positive revealed law, certainly forbid. By first separating them from the other races of mankind, by giving to them a widely diverse physical and mental constitution, by impressing their very natures with a feeling of inferiority and a spirit of submission and dependence, and by a marked distinction of color, which the Scriptures themselves declare to be unchangeable, the Great Author of all created beings has declared that whatever human law may enjoin, or infidel fanaticism may inculcate, the line of demarkation is too clearly drawn ever to be obliterated. They are, however, a branch of the human family, descended from the same common parents with ourselves, and subjected to the same destiny. With us they fell from a primitive state of purity and innocence, and with us they are embraced in the covenant of grace and mercy. Many of them already cherish in their hearts those precious truths and doctrines which console and sustain us amid the trials and sorrows of life, and with us they look forward, beyond this scene of things, to a state of unending joy and felicity at God's right hand. Placed as they now are in our midst, so ignorant, so helpless and dependent, it is our imperative duty to extend to them that christian charity and sympathy due from christian men to christian men, to aid and encourage them in every good word and work, and to afford to all those yet exposed to the wrath to come, the means of spiritual life.

Since your last meeting, the General Association of Virginia and the Southern Baptist Convention have both held their regular meetings, and have acted with entire unanimity on this subject. In harmony with the advice of these bodies, as well as in furtherance of the resolutions passed at your last anniversary, your Committee would recommend—

That every possible facility be afforded to the colored people within the bounds of this Association hearing regularly the preached word—

That they be received into the communion and fellowship of our Churches as heretofore—

That when numbers and christian efficiency justify, and circumstances demand, they should be formed into distinct churches and congregations—

That, in their present destitute condition, they should be allowed the use of our houses of worship, under proper restrictions, until they can provide houses of their own—

That they be allowed representation in our Association by white delegates chosen from among the membership of churches connected with this body—

That efforts be made to provide them with an efficient and intelligent Ministry of their own race—

That they be taught in Sabbath Schools and Bible Classes, and afforded all the means possible of improving their knowledge of the Scriptures.

Your committee, with the lights now before them, cannot go further than this, and recommend the formation of Colored Associations within the bounds of this Association. That the conditions and wants of Colored churches may make such organizations desirable and necessary at no distant day, there can be no question. But in the present state of things, the congregating of colored persons in such large numbers as would, in all probability, attend such meetings, would constitute a most serious objection to such organizations. In the first place, they have not the means among themselves of sustaining the delegates and visitors to such bodies; and in the second place, any neighborhood would object to an assemblage of the kind in their midst. The prejudices of race would most probably be most deeply aroused by such gatherings, and break forth in flagrant acts and excesses most injurious to the peace and good order of society, scandalous to religion, and dangerous to the highest temporal interest of both classes. When the two races shall have recovered in a measure from the terrible shock which both have received, and society has become fixed and stable under the new order of things, then we may venture to advise such measures; but for the present, let us be satisfied to train them, as best we can, for the duties which now especially devolve upon them as members of individual churches, that they may be the better prepared for higher and more enlarged spheres of christian obligation and usefulness in the rapidly approaching future, when such responsibilities can no longer be deferred.

Respectfully submitted,
Chas. L. Cocke

The report, after much discussion and many suggestions, all indicating a deep and general interest on the subject, was unanimously adopted.

On motion, the application of Enon Colored Church for membership was considered and by unanimous vote the Church received into the Association, and the Moderator gave to her delegates the right hand of fellowship.

In 1868 Enon reported 106 members and Enon (Colored) 133. In 1869:

On motion, Enon Colored Church was regarded as being dismissed from this Association, she having joined a colored association.

Mary Bishop wrote another article:

Church Gives Thanks for Gift of Hope

Soon, there'll be a paved Moriah Lane, courtesy of the city of Roanoke. Already, friends of Mount Moriah Baptist Church have given it two new bathrooms and a refurbished kitchen. Members of the 135-year-old church held open house this past weekend to thank the nearly 200 individuals, churches, organizations and businesses who gave money, materials, and new hope to one of the Roanoke Valley's oldest churches.

Louise Witt, who with her husband, Silas, led the improvement effort, reeled off thank-yous—a long, long list. "Please thank the people who donated throughout Virginia, South Carolina, Philadelphia, Pa., and Washington, D.C.," she said Sunday afternoon, as visitors dropped by the fellowship hall. "I've been so happy, I don't know what to do," she said. "I say, Thank you Jesus."

She was grateful to Roanoke Mayor David Bowers, who came by Saturday to proclaim it "Mount Moriah Day." She expressed thanks to Ethel Smith, a Virginia Tech instructor and writer of local black history, who put the word out about the church's need.

It tickled Witt that a television report Saturday night included audio of one of Mount Moriah's two toilets flushing furiously—music to members' ears. Mount Moriah's membership has dwindled to about a dozen, partly because elderly worshipers were unable to walk to the outdoor toilet behind the church. And the church couldn't serve food because it had no water in the kitchen. Already, more people are coming to church. Sunday's visitors included Leola Alexander Burford of Christiansburg, who turns 99 on July 31. She's the aunt of Louise Curtis Thompson, clerk of the church for more than 30 years.

Churches sent choir robes and hymnals. There's a new water fountain, a new heater. Some donors—such as the business that gave new kitchen cabinets and sink—did so anonymously. Some people sent $3 or $5; the largest donation, $300, came from a small church. It was the little churches—about 20 of them—and not the big churches that answered Mount Moriah's call for plumbing.

Mount Moriah is waiting to hear if it will be declared a historic site. The congregation was founded by slaves in 1858. The current sanctuary, built in 1873, sits on a hilltop just off of U.S. 460 near the Roanoke County line.

This year's homecoming service and lunch on July 25 should be one of the best ever, Witt said. "We're going to celebrate and drink cold water on the hill."[6]

The following is the final article that Mary Bishop wrote in her series about the Mount Moriah Church:

Old Building, New Landmarks
Baptist Church, New River Home Make Registry

Two years ago, the white clapboard church on the hill was enduring, its roots still dug deep. Water was needed for indoor plumbing, though, so the church could grow a little. Its sanctuary was built in 1873. A donation drive produced two bathrooms, a refurbished kitchen, a water fountain and a paved drive less than a year later. Wednesday, Mount Moriah Baptist Church—which began as a thatched-roof, open-air shelter that slaves fashioned African-style around 1858—received more good news. The church, located near the Roanoke County line off U.S. 460, was formally added to the Virginia Landmarks Registry. "I'm elated. It's been an uphill struggle, but now we can keep the doors open," said Louise Curtis Thompson when told of the news Wednesday afternoon. "We were worried at one point a few years ago, when someone tried to buy the land next to the church." Thompson has told the church, with a working congregation of 12 members, it has plans to open for visitors at least one day a week.

Deborah Woodward, an assistant with the Virginia Department of Historic Resources, said the state designation "draws importance" to a property's significance in a community for planning educational purposes. The action doesn't restrict a property owner in any way and opens the door to possible state preservation-grant funds and technical assistance, she said.

The Virginia Historic Resources Board also voted this week to recommend that Mount Moriah be added to the National Register of Historic Places. This recommendation will be acted on at the national level later, according to Deborah Woodward of the Virginia Department of Historic Resources.[7]

Mary Bishop, Reverend Alvord Beardsless of Hollins College, and I attended services at Mount Moriah the following Sunday. Reverend Beardsless was particularly interested in the church since its history related to the founder of Hollins College. Once he had learned of Charles Cocke's comments regretting the fact of slavery, Reverend Beardsless had made the assumption that Cocke hadn't been a slaveholder. Although I was surprised that Reverend Beardsless could have actually believed this, I did have to rethink Charles Lewis Cocke myself. During my research I had only thought of him indirectly, but the soft-spoken, steady voice of Louise Witt insisted that I expand my assessment of Cocke. "He had to be a nice man to educate his slaves." Sometimes that statement made no sense to me at all, but other times I thought that Mrs. Witt made an important point.

I researched other slaveholders who had educated the persons they enslaved. The most interesting example I found was in Mississippi. Joseph Emory Davis, one of Jefferson Davis's older brothers, educated Benjamin Montgomery, whom he purchased in 1836. Apparently Joseph Davis recognized the intellectual potential of Mr. Montgomery; he offered him the use of his library and then proceeded to watch him improve his reading skills. In fact, Montgomery invented a steamboat propeller that Jefferson Davis tried to register in Montgomery's name in Washington, D.C., only to be told that a slave couldn't be issued a patent. Supposedly, all of the slaves in the area came to live on Montgomery's land, which eventually was called Montgomery Bend. As a result, Montgomery became one of the wealthiest landowners in Mississippi.[8]

I had always been treated well by the members of Mount Moriah, and I was thankful because I thought I had found another church home in the Roanoke area. But on the Sunday that Reverend Beardsless attended services with us, I immediately became invisible to them. I felt totally ignored. Their attention was devoted to pleasing Reverend Beardsless. But the hurt and disappointment would eventually let go of me. My feelings had to be placed in an intellectual context, not an emotional one—even though it was difficult.

I lunched with Anna Lawson the next week. We talked and talked about the situation. I realized that Mount Moriah had offered me yet another challenge. Those church members were not used to interacting with whites socially. A white person had probably never attended their services. And they were used to pleasing whites if for no other reason than tradition. They were folks of their time. The narratives of the slave systems were many and complicated. The more involved I became in my work, the more overwhelmed I grew. This institution of slavery had left our country scarred in places we didn't even realize had been hurt. I was not hopeful for the possibility of healing; the pain and human cost seemed too deep for me.

Other Voices of Silence

> The past is all that makes the present
> coherent, and the past will remain hor-
> rible as long as we refuse to assess it
> honestly.
>
> James Baldwin

After Leslie Taylor, a reporter for the Roanoke Times and World News, wrote an article for the paper's Saturday edition about my work on the Hollins Community, I was surprised and amazed at how much support came my way. I received photographs, telephone calls, letters, and even a book that had been written about the folks in the community in 1910.

I received in the mail, wrapped in plain brown paper, an autographed copy of Which One? And Other Ante Bellum Days, by Mary M. Pleasants, who had taught music at the college and was a member of the Cocke family. I was nervous when I opened the book. It had been a Christmas gift to a Mrs. E. V. Gorkin and was signed with the warm regards of the author.

I had no expectations about the book; I assumed it would give me some insight into the era of my work. It did. During my research, I was constantly reminded that my work was in another time and that I could not apply to the past our late-twentieth-century ways of being. Otherwise, I would spend too much time being angry and depressed. The preface of the book reads:

> As a book without a preface resembles a house without a portico, I shall not send my loving tribute to the old-time mammy and butler without a few words of explanation of its appearance at this time.
>
> Although books which purport to depict the character of the *ante bellum*, trusted, slaves of the South, are numerous, there are very few of them which give *true pictures* of the house-servants of those days, and there is consequent need of additions to the genuine class. Therefore, both from the experiences of my friends and from my own life, I have collected four striking types of house-servants to perpetuate in print, for the enlightenment of future generations, *what was the real, ante bellum, family slave.*

I was reminded of the time when the film Birth of a Nation *was shown at the White House during the presidency of Woodrow Wilson. African Americans were excited that black folks would finally have their debut on the silver screen. But how disappointed, frustrated, and sad they were after the showing of the film, to know what whites really thought of them. I shared their feelings after reading the preface, but I continued to read the first chapter, which went on:*

> Since Thackeray, in The Diary of C. Jeames de la Pluche, and Dickens, in the novel utterances of Samuel Weller, have immortalized the English dialect of valets, I have always been much interested in the peculiarities of speech of all lower classes of people. In America, where a cosmopolitan population furnishes the dialects of the Chinaman, Irishman, Dutchman, Frenchman, and, indeed, what not, there is a fine opportunity to indulge my proclivity. But of all the mongrel English spoken in the United States, the speech of the ante bellum negro of the South combines both most attraction in its musical simplicity of language and union of humor and pathos.

I put the book down and didn't pick it up again for years, when I moved to a different state. I resumed where I had left off, and I didn't put it down until I had completed all of the seventy-four pages. I am not sure I understood what I had read; the text was in a dialect that I didn't readily pick up. I wasn't as negatively affected as I had been earlier, and I was very thankful for the photographs of Aunt Cindy, Dusty Plotter Frank, Mammy Jane, and Mammy Patsy, all of whom worked at the college at some point in their lives.

With all the support people were giving me, I felt courageous and had a new belief in my work. There were many calls from alumnae, many of whom remembered Mr. Lewis Hunt especially, as he was the head waiter when they were students. All were happy to see that something was being done in his honor, and they believed that the folks of the Hollins Community should have long been remembered before now.

I even received more telephone calls with offers of photographs from members of the community. Never any stories, however.

I thought and hoped that perhaps healing was possible. Maybe history was the answer. But then I thought, no, that was the problem—Americans have not been taught a complete history. History is from a perspective; therefore, it is not really possible to discover an objective truth about the past. In this case, the majority perspective is limited, subjective, guilty, ashamed, judgmental, in denial, and selfish. Overlooked or repressed past realities remain a mystery. And it's that compelling aspect of it that interested me. The mysterious worlds of Hollins College and the Hollins Community—the hidden and silent narratives of slavery.

We are accustomed to slavery being represented with the "big house," "field hands," other "servants," "master," and "mistress." But there were many forms of slavery, and they have conveniently disappeared without acknowledgment,

The "old kitchen," 1952. Photo in collection of the author.

like the Hollins Community. History comprises what is known about the past. I come up blanks when I raise questions: How do we paint a true picture of the past? Is it possible? How do we offer a voice to a world of silence? What is the human cost when we don't make the effort?

I talked with friends and colleagues on the subject of silence. I read books. I also remembered a woman who camed up to me after I had presented a lecture on the Hollins Community for the Virginia Foundation for Public Policy and the Humanities in Charlottesville. She simply slipped me a piece of paper with her name and telephone number written on it. She also told me that she had lived in the Hollins Community and wanted very much to talk to me.

I accepted her offer. I interviewed Ann Jones-Smith at her home in Charlottesville, Virginia.

"Where exactly in the community is or was your house?" I asked.

"If you'd look down on the older area of Hollins, and look up the hill is where our house is. We were not exactly part of the community. Folks used to consider our house to be right above the community. I have no idea whom they bought the land from. It was maybe thirteen or fourteen acres of land that they built their dream house on."

"Do you have any idea regarding what they paid for the house?"

"I can remember them talking about it. There were five or six bedrooms, a full basement, living room, family room, large kitchen, dining room, and another room to eat in. It was a huge house. I believe they paid thirty-six thousand dollars for it. I recall when the house was being built, my dad would take me—I was a daddy's girl—out there to watch them excavate the land. I got to ride on the bulldozers. We saw it from the beginning, when they first started clearing out the land and laying the foundation, until the house was built. I still dream about that house. My memories are vivid about it. I remember the house wasn't even completed, but Mom and Dad would go out to do some work. Dad stayed the night sometimes, and I stayed with him. My sister would go back into town with my mom. It was a real bond for us. It must have been about the time I turned eight that we moved into the house; that would have made the time 1959. For the first two years that we lived there instead of going to the school where I should have gone we would ride a bus all the way to Fincastle, which was the only black school. Since my aunt was the principal at the elementary school in Roanoke, my mother got permission for us to attend Lincoln Terrace Elementary School."

"Was the school affiliated with Lucy Addison?"

"Lucy Addison was the high school, and then there was a junior high school. This was all in the part of what was called 'the projects.' Lincoln Terrace was a brand new school and my aunt got the principalship there. We went there for two years. I think what happened is somewhere between the end of the fourth grade and starting fifth grade, my sister and I had gone for free, and the city was going to charge us. Whatever happened, my parents decided we would go to the school in Fincastle instead of staying in the Roanoke school. We went to Central Academy. For a little while it was just my sister, me, and the Johnsons and the Meades. The Crowders and the Brewsters lived in Roanoke County. I remember meeting them and riding on the school bus with them. It took us forty-five minutes to get to school. We would pass two or three elementary schools on the way. Our house was built on that side of the mountain [Tinker Mountain]. My parents were so used to their community of friends and associates in the city of Roanoke that we still attended church there, rather than the one in the Hollins Community."

"How old were you when your family first attended the Hollins First Baptist Church?"

"If memory serves me, I was fourteen when we started attending the church in Hollins. One of the reasons was that my mother had high blood pressure—not diabetic—and developed blood clots and had to have her leg amputated. As a result, there was some trauma in the family. My father was an alcoholic. I can remember he and Mama fighting one night, and her blood pressure went up so high. At first she called the doctor and complained that her leg was hurting. Instead of him coming to visit—because in those days doctors did make house calls—he kept prescribing things over the phone, until the day she had to go to the hospital. Because her blood pressure was so high, the clots developed, and she had to have her leg amputated. It was hard to see that, but the turnaround was unbelievable; my dad became a whole new person. He truly loved Mama; after this happened, he never drank again. I think he started going to church at Hollins because the church in Roanoke was one of those old black Baptist churches that had fifty steps just from the main street. And there were more steps to get to the church. The First Baptist Church in Roanoke's old building is still there, even though they built a new church. So my parents decided we would start going to the church in Hollins. It was closer, easier, and more accessible for Mama. That ended up being a wonderful experience. My sister and I got to meet more people in the community, especially on the Roanoke County side of Hollins. As a teenager I was part of the church youth group and Sunday school, which was really my social life. I was a Girl Scout. I know Miss Emma [Bruce] and her sister Alice were scout leaders. The last couple of years before I graduated from high school, I was a junior superintendent of Sunday school. Of course, Miss Emma was the superintendent. Mama was a deaconess in church and Daddy became a deacon. It was a good relationship, but I still felt distant. But as a child I always felt distant from everyone, like I didn't fit in."

"If you're the family or person who moves into a community where everyone else was born into, you're bound to feel like an outsider. Since your family moved in, it's probably clearer to you today."

"I would imagine soon after going to church is when other friends, the Joneses came. Reverend Jones lived in the community. He was a widow and had three children: two sons and a daughter."

"When did you first know about the community's history?"

"I guess I sort of always knew about it because I knew everyone worked for Hollins College except my father and Mr. Jones. Everyone else's mama, daddy, grandparents, uncles, aunts, and cousins worked for the college. I didn't necessarily know what type of work they did."

"Do you have any memory of ever going on campus?"

"The only time I went to the campus was when a friend, Cynthia Hale, was a student there. When I was finally able to drive, I practiced on the grounds of the campus. Where our house was located, we could look over and see the grounds. Of course, Hollins College had this traditional Tinker Day, when the girls would dress up in costumes and climb to the top of the mountain and perform skits. We used to watch because of all the noise and excitement on the mountain. One time I think a campfire started a blaze. We had to be careful going up and down the driveway because the students would walk up our driveway and cut onto the path that went up the mountain. That's about the only connection that I had with Hollins College."

"When in your adult life did it occur to you about the community's relationship to slavery?"

"I guess probably in my late twenties or early thirties. I moved to Charlottesville and all of a sudden I realized the control that universities and colleges have over the black communities, who generally served them, and the towns around them. I feel that way about the University of Virginia and Charlottesville. I thought about the communities as a whole and how it was so easy for any hiring institution, like the University of Virginia, to keep the black community down because those institutions are often the only place to work. 'We won't educate you, but as long as you are a good little servant we will pay you minimum wages and promise you that when you retire you'll get thus and so.' A lot of people talked about their grand jobs at Hollins. I remember Carole's dad, Dave Bruce [Emma Bruce's brother], used to drive a big Cadillac all the time. Everyone assumed that was from the money he earned. He probably worked himself to death for a Cadillac, which probably cost five or six thousand dollars. But folks were led to believe that everyone who worked at the college was well off."

"Their ancestors were probably better off. It seems to me that each generation of black folks who worked at the college grew poorer—if you think about life during the Depression and other hard times the country has endured."

"It's sad when you think about it. They [the community residents] are good people, but there was no sense of value other than a high school diploma for most of the kids who grew up there. I am thinking of Bernard Harris, who was so tall and was to receive a basketball scholarship. I don't know if he even graduated from high school. There were others, like Cora Lewis, who was Harry Smith's sister. She was part of that community. Her oldest son went into the military. He received training that way. I remember that most of the guys my age went into the military. Mostly the navy, and a few went into the army. Even some of the girls did that. I think my sister and I were the only two who went to college, other than the Jones's kids. It was all about a value system. But the community hasn't grown beyond what they were twenty to thirty years ago. So it appears on those rare occasions that I go back."

"From what high school did you graduate?"

"Lord Botetourt. So did Peggy Johnson and Helen Meade. We were the three from Hollins who graduated from Lord Botetourt in 1969. Carole Coles, David Bruce's daughter, graduated from Northside that year. Of course the schools were rivals because Bernard Harris's family lived near the main intersection going toward Route 11. They built the oil refinery next to it.

"Every time I visit, there's more and more commerce. Mrs. Bruce and Mr. Harry Smith are the oldest members of the community. She's eighty-eight and he's eighty-three. I believe it's just going to be a matter of time until they're all gone. Young folks don't stay any longer. Of course, there's no reason to.

"I know that for a time the Minnises, including Wade and Andrew, brothers my age, lived in a little house kitty-corned to the baseball field. Hazeltine Johnson's family—Monroe Johnson was her father, and she had a sister, Louise, that was my age—lived in a house across from the old school. I think it's gone now. That old school was our recreation center. We would go there in the summer and do things when we weren't in church. Even then, Mama didn't let us go so often. I don't know if it was because she didn't know the people that well."

"If you as a child felt like an outsider, I am sure your mother felt it."

"I remember that the families were very close-knit and protective of one another. If you said or did anything to them or someone's brother, sister, or cousin everybody would come after you. They defended each other. Sometimes I felt that my family was viewed as the 'people on the hill.' They considered us to be better off. I believe that this was perpetuated by Hollins College. I now understand that the mentality is related to slavery."

"Did members of the community visit you? Kids?"

"Our visitors would be family and relatives. The Jones's kids would come up to the house and visit. Maybe a few times Peggy and Carole came up to the house, but that was really it. We weren't allowed to visit any of the other houses except Peggy and Carole's."

"Why?"

"I don't know. It was just a family rule. And as children we did what we were told."

"How long did your family live in that house?"

"Until 1972. They moved back to Roanoke, off of Hershberger Road. I don't know why."

"Is the house still there?"

"As far as I know. Every time I drive on Interstate 81, I look for that house. When I go back I am always tempted to go and knock on the door. I remember the people who bought the house from my parents were retired military, and they were white. I don't think any other black family ever lived in that house again. They welcomed us to come and visit. I think we visited a couple of times, but after they sold it we lost track of the owners. When we went home last summer for my family reunion, Morgan [Ann's daughter] and I went to church at Hollins. Everybody was just so glad to see us."

"Why is it different now?"

"I don't know why I didn't feel the friendliness and openness when I was growing up. They always make us feel welcome now. Rev. and Mrs. Jones's old-est son, Charles Calloway, is now the minister at the First Baptist Church in Hollins. I had a crush on him. They're from down between Bedford and Forest. Reverend Jones was acting minister there at one time. That was after Reverend Keaton left. The irony of it is that when we joined the church in Hollins, Reverend E. G. Hall was the pastor there, and when I moved to Charlottesville, Reverend E. G. Hall was here. Everyone asked me why I didn't join his church. I said, 'I grew up with Reverend Hall.' When I go back now I feel a genuine warmth. Everyone had kids sooner than I did. I remember faces; I'm not good with names. Once they told me their names I could make the connection."

"Do you remember your parents making any reference to the college when you were growing up? Or was it thought of as simply a place to work?"

"I'm sure my father did some moving jobs there. Mom didn't work, so any connections she had would have come from the missionary circles or dea-conesses. It's interesting to sit here today and think about how it was."

"Do you remember any specific friends from the community? And what hap-pened to them?"

"I think Carole went to Norfolk State for a year or two. But of the ones who graduated that year, I am the only one who went to college."

"Where did you attend college?"

"I went to Radford University but wanted to attend Hampton University. The guidance counselor told me as a junior that it cost a lot of money, and she didn't think that my parents could have afforded it. She didn't say, 'If you really want to go, let's see if we can find a way to make it happen.' Radford was looking for minorities at the time. The guidance counselor also told me that Radford was willing to give me X amount of money, and it wouldn't be so hard on my parents.

"I can remember when I would come home from college, and we would hang out together. The boy's name, I am thinking of, is Andrew Mennis, and his brother is Wade, who married a girl name Anna, from Fincastle. Maybe because I attended Lord Botetourt High School I felt distance from them later. But also my high school has never invited me to a class reunion. Maybe if we had lived on the Roanoke County part of the community, I would feel closer to them. Also there were more African American students who lived on that part of Hollins."

"Have you contacted your high school to give them your address?"

"No. The thing is, they have means of contacting my sister, who graduated after I did. Once we graduated from high school, it wasn't long afterwards that we moved. I guess they didn't keep track of things as well as they do now."

"Maybe you should drop them a postcard with your address, telephone number, and the year you graduated. What else do you remember about the community?"

"I can remember during my college years that I would always enjoy the third Sunday in July because that was homecoming for the First Baptist Church at Hollins. Everybody came home for that. All of the adults would go in the church and the kids would hang around outside because the old church was too small for everyone to sit. We always talked about Lily Mae Patterson; she could sing better than anybody else in the world. One homecoming, she sang 'How Great Thou Art'; she cracked the stained glass window at the old church. I will never forget that. Even when people see me now, we talk about that. As kids we used to imitate her. We didn't appreciate that she had a gift of a very strong voice."

"Are there others?"

"It bothers me when I think about folks like Helen Meade, who was much more academically gifted than I was. Pam Meade's sister. Pam is the baby."

"Did you realize that Pam Meade is the only young woman from the community to have graduated from Hollins?"

"I had no idea. I recall that Helen had a child when she was in the eleventh grade. She probably doesn't live out there now. I wonder when I see the people coming to church, how many of them actually live in the community or live in Roanoke."

"My students are always surprised when I share statistics with them regarding the fact that most of the people who work in this country are the working poor. And it's not that they are surprised by these folks, they just ignore them. But they are the folks who come in at night and clean the classrooms, or the person who takes their order at McDonald's. They are the folks who work at Hollins by day and somewhere else by night to make ends meet."

"It makes me wonder why it is that a college that has as much as Hollins— why don't they pay their employees so that they won't have to work two or three jobs. Why don't they provide opportunities for all of their employees to better themselves? People just don't want to open their eyes. You know that slavery is part of their history. How else would they have survived?"

"The more important issue for me, is how the college is serving the community today. Mrs. Bruce worked there for forty-six years. She shouldn't have to clean three houses a week for a living today."

"With all of those years at Hollins, she should have retired with an income and other benefits. A part of slavery is getting people to work for little or no money, and never never encouraging anyone to do better or to become educated. The message was clear: 'This is all that you can do, and as soon as your children are old enough, they, too, can work here.' I considered myself very blessed because my mother was a trained educator and encouraged us to reach higher. Both of my parents were domestic workers at some point. I could have easily been in the same situation as many of the young folks in Hollins.

"I am thinking about Thomas Jefferson and Monticello. I heard on the news that some of the descendants of Sally Hemings have been invited to attend a meeting of the Jefferson descendants. It would be interesting to know how many of the people in Hollins are descendants of the founder of the college."

"That's a valid question. There's one photograph of Mr. Lewis Hunt, who's very dark skinned, and his wife, who is so fair she looks white. From that photograph, it was clear that he was considered to be the 'HNIC' [Head Negro In Charge]. He called himself 'Dean of Servants.' It was not an official title. You look at his wife's photograph and also know that she is at least half white. It was a very isolated area. And like you've already said, there was a sense of not being open to outsiders, since they had some of the best jobs for that time."

"I guess having lived here and understanding the slave mentality, I can transfer it back to Hollins and it's so much clearer. It's good for me to reflect because it helps me to understand why the situation was the way it was at Hollins when I was a child. They thought that my sister and I were spoiled because we didn't have to work at the college. I never knew why my parents bought land there."

"It was the late fifties, which meant that possibly it could have been one of the few places they could actually buy land."

"I wonder—after your book is published, will anyone from the community have another story to tell—or take the initiative and dig a little deeper."

"I hope so. Slavery is difficult to discuss and think about. There's too much dishonesty in this country about it. Most of the resistance I get from students when teaching the slave narratives, for example, are from African American students. If I am teaching a class of thirty-five students, three of whom are African Americans, the message I receive from the black students is that they are embarrassed and wish I would drop dead. And the white students are defensive and in denial. I, or a book, cannot give dignity to the folks in the community; they must claim it. My message is simple: They and their ancestors worked for more than 150 years for Hollins College, and they deserve to be acknowledged and recorded in history."

"If taken that way, it would probably shed a whole different light on the next generation. I would hate to think that one day I would go to First Baptist Church Hollins and there's no one there that I have a connection with. The cemetery across the street is grown over. Nothing is there anymore that reminds me of the past. The last time I sent Miss Emma a message for Christmas, she sent me a whole newspaper article about her. She doesn't change. I forget how old she is because she looks the same.

Ann Jones-Smith, April 1999. Photo by the author.

"I am reading a book now about a woman who did research on domestic workers. It's awesome. As soon I started to read it, I remembered how Mama and Daddy used to talk about the people they worked for."

"Only Mrs. Bruce and Mr. Smith have been willing to talk to me for the most part."

"The others have believed that their purpose in life was to serve."

"Asking someone to share their life story with someone they don't know is a bit much. And after all, I am an outsider, and a black woman writing a book. That must be an odd concept to most of them."

"The last time I attended church there was last summer. The preacher asked for a special prayer for one of my first boyfriends. Apparently his life had gone downhill. He was in the hospital. I think of the guys, and so many of them didn't do well. Vietnam messed up a lot of them my age. And there was drugs in Roanoke as well."

The following Saturday morning I listened to National Public Radio, as I generally do if I am home and not talking on the telephone. This day, the host was interviewing Edward Ball, a reporter from New York whose father, an Episcopal clergyman, died when Edward was twelve. His father gave him a copy of a "Ball Family" history and said to him, "One day you'll want to know about all of this." It was a description of the family's more than twenty antebellum plantations along the Cooper River in South Carolina, where four thousand slaves had toiled.

Years later, Edward Ball attended a family reunion of his white family members. They were steeped in plantation pride. Reacting to his family's indifference to its slaveholding history, he found himself with a personal mission to discover the part of his family's plantation history that had not been recounted—the lives of the slaves. The book that resulted from his discoveries is titled Slaves in the Family.

He researched the stories of the blacks who had suffered bondage to the Ball family. For many years, he looked for their descendants. "The progeny of slaves and the property owners are forever linked," he said. "We have been in each other's lives. We have been in each other's dreams. We have been in each other's beds."

He approached many living descendants of the persons the Ball family had enslaved, which could have been as many as a hundred thousand. He was sure that some were related to him through the miscegenation of his forefathers. His research was overwhelming because enslaved persons were recorded as property and had no last names until after the Civil War. And, of course, they were discouraged from taking the name Ball.

He followed all his leads, the most important being the Ball surname and his family's extensive plantation records documenting its slave-trading activity and even some slave rebellions.

Edward Ball contacted and developed friendly relationships with some of the descendants of his ancestors' African American slaves. He described a memorable moment when he met with Emily Frayer, who was born in a cabin on one of the Ball plantations. She hadn't seen the cabin since childhood. When Ball took her there to visit, she passed up the opportunity to see the "big house" to search for the cabin, which they found, discovering that it is now a chicken house. But she was happy to see it again. Edward Ball told her, "I am sorry for what my family did to your family." And she replied, "I thank you. You come right on time."

I was speechless for many moments after the interview. In Mrs. Frayer, I heard the voice of Mrs. Bruce. I heard the voice of Mrs. Witt. I heard the voice of Mrs. Thompson. I heard the voices of my mother and grandmother. I heard the voices of black women all over the world whose voices have been numbed by silence. I knew that I could never record the unrecorded, but by listening to the power of these women, I was sure that I could offer voice to the silence of the Hollins Community and Hollins College.

I found many photographs but was usually unable to associate them with a name. I offer them here, deferring humbly to the voices of silence.

Unidentified Hollins Community residents. Photo
from Zackery Hunt; in collection of the author.

Alease Meade, 1955, mother of Pamela
Meade, first Hollins Community resident
to graduate from Hollins. Photo from
Zackery Hunt; in collection of the author.

Glady Moore. Photo from Zackery Hunt; in collection of the author.

"Mammy Jane." In Mary M. Pleasants, *Which One? and Other Ante Bellum Days* (Boston: James H. Early, 1910).

"Mammy Patsy." In Pleasants, *Which One?*

"Dusky Plotter Frank." In Pleasants, *Which One?*

Unidentified woman. In Pleasants, *Which One?*

"Aunt Cindy." West Building in background. In Pleasants, *Which One?*

10

President in a Pot

They have killed the
spirits of so many people.
They have left a
place and ended up in a
destination without understanding
the route they took.
Esther Vasser

All during my research and interviews with folks at Hollins College and the Hollins Community, the name Esther Vassar kept popping up. Later I learned that she was one of two African American faculty members that the college had ever hired. In the community, she had become a near legend. I assumed that she had taught at the college for years and was now retired and living in Richmond, Virginia. However, I thought it was odd that the college didn't have an address or a telephone number for her.

Finally, after three years, I met someone who knew her and gave me her address and telephone number. In fact, Opal Moore was a friend of hers. I tried to get an interview with her, which took another year since she was traveling back and forth to South Africa as an ambassador for the state of Virginia.

Late one night at the end of February 1997, Opal Moore telephoned me with news from Ms. Vassar. She had told Opal that if I wanted to interview her I'd better get to Richmond because there was a possibility that she would be in South Africa for the next two years. Her timing was excellent; my spring break had just started. Needless to say, I dropped everything, threw clothes in my car, and headed to Richmond via Roanoke to pick up Opal Moore. She had agreed to travel with me.

When we arrived at Ms. Vassar's home, her teenage daughter greeted us and said her mother would be home soon. Immediately, I knew something was wrong with my assumptions about Ms. Vassar. Her daughter was perhaps eight years younger than my son. About ten minutes later a sassy, spirited woman wearing a miniskirt strutted through the door. And that was Esther Vassar!

This interview was conducted on March 1, 1997, at the home of Esther Vassar in Richmond, Virginia.

"How long were you employed at Hollins College?"

"One year."

"When were you there?"

"I believe it was 1971 or 1972."

"How did you come to be there?"

"Well, I was living in Charlottesville, having gone there to graduate school [at the University of Virginia]. It was a year before I received my master's degree and I had just gotten married. My husband was interviewing for a job with the Legal Aid Society in Roanoke. In the course of going down there for the interview, we thought about me getting a job as well. So, I saw an exit that said Hollins College. I suggested we stop there; maybe it was a good place. We pulled off the expressway and drove to the college. Weeping willow trees greeted us as we arrived on campus. We parked in the parking lot and I thought, 'No, I don't think so,' after looking at the college. We were about to get back in the car and leave when an African American student saw us and literally stopped us."

"Why did you think, 'No, I don't think so?'"

"Because it didn't seem like a place that would need me. We were getting ready to leave and the student came by the parking lot and stopped us and asked, 'Excuse me, but do you need help?' When we said no, she said, literally asked, 'Are you looking for a job?' I answered, 'Well, I don't know.' She escorted us to Dean Wheeler's office. I had my résumé because I had come prepared to find a job. We talked. Afterwards, he showed us around campus and pointed out a house where we could live. Based on my experiences and being qualified, he indicated that they wanted me to work there. We negotiated the terms. I was hired as assistant dean of students. But I insisted that I teach a course in the English department, because I was experienced and I believe in an academic institution one should always teach. It was agreed that I teach a course beginning the second semester."

"What did you teach?"

"I taught African American literature in the English department. My husband and I went back to Charlottesville with jobs."

"Tell me more about the class you taught."

"I taught an upper-level class with a couple of graduate students. The class was good because the students were so hungry for information about race."

"Who were the students?"

"I don't remember. I don't even remember the textbooks I used. How am I supposed to remember twenty-six years ago? If I could find my syllabus; that would take some searching. Plus everything was so new. I relied heavily on outside resources. You're talking about a program that didn't have a budget because when I arrived the budget had already been established. Money was taken from someplace else. The college could never have afforded Ossie Davis, even today. It was a time when you could appeal to people based on need. It was before agents and such. I called Ossie Davis at his home."

"Was Dean Wheeler in a position to offer you a position that day just by the interview without consulting a committee?"

"Verbally, in terms of the offer, yes. I received a follow-up letter later. I had my résumé, and he was able to make the decision. And they needed somebody. I think at that time, they had a part-time woman who also worked in Roanoke. She came certain days to act as an advisor for the minority students."

"When you say they needed somebody, do you mean a black person?"

"Yes."

"Was the part-time woman in Roanoke black?"

"Yes."

"Were you aware that you were the only black faculty member at the college? How many African American students were enrolled in the college? Did you have other responsibilities?"

"They indicated to me when I first interviewed. I think there were approximately thirty black students. The numbers were heavy in the freshman year because of recruitment efforts. I volunteered to serve as a recruiter for the college as well. I went to several college fairs around the country. I sat on the admissions committee. And I performed all of the many things that an administrator would normally do."

"How do you think you were perceived or received by the faculty members?"

"I did not have any problems. I remember one funny incident, however. It wasn't any different then than it would be now. One of the faculty members came to me. I don't remember who she was. 'Esther, I need to talk to you. I have this black student in my class and don't quite know how to teach her.' I said, 'You know, I've got a similar problem. I have these white students in my class . . .' She got the point. The irony was that here I was there alone, a minority faculty member, in a college that was predominantly white, and she had this one black student and the rest of the world was hers. And there I was in an alien world with all of the students except a few blacks, and I was supposed to give her coping strategy for dealing with that one child. Nobody gave me coping strategies; I developed them. But I said I've got this, too. Kind of like swapping dreams in a folktale. We just swapped problems and it took care of itself. I didn't give her any strategies and she couldn't offer me any."

"Did you go to Hollins College with intentions of staying more than a year?"

"It was a first job for my husband. We had a choice of coming to Richmond, ironically, or going to Roanoke. Based on the facts that I had a job, and we didn't know much about Richmond, we chose Roanoke."

"Why did you leave after one year?"

"We left because my husband got a job with the subway system, the union that was building the subway system in Washington, D.C. It was an opportunity for me to go back to D.C. I had gone to undergraduate school at Howard University. One of my former professors chaired the English department. I called, got an interview, and spent four years there."

"When did you first learn about the members of the Hollins Community?"

"Well, I always talked to the maids and service people for lots of reasons. One, because usually they look like me, and secondly because they can be a lot of help. They usually end up being my best friends and closest allies. I got to know them in a natural sense. Plus my presence offered them pride in a natural sense. They would speak to me and always express happiness. I was receptive to that. They invited me to church. With those connections I became friends with them."

"When did you learn that their ancestors had been enslaved at the college?"

"Well, I started asking questions about where they lived. They all came from the one area—'Oldfields.' I knew that the college was established before Emancipation. The set-up interested me. I suspected as much. Then I did some research on my own. As assistant dean of students, I also assumed that one of my duties was to diversify—before the term was used—the campus. I invited my friends, who happened to be Houston Baker and Ossie Davis, to come to Hollins College to speak. I extended invitations to the maids and janitors and members of the church. They came happily. Ossie Davis did an interview with the black radio station. He slept in housing on campus. For those who couldn't attend his presentation, we transmitted his speech over the radio. We also had Joseph Washington, a black religious scholar, who is well known. He married my husband and me. I had this whole list of impressive people. When you've got Ossie Davis, Houston Baker, and Joe Washington, you've got a year's program already. And there were others. It was an interesting year."

"How were the African American students treated by the college? Can you offer specific examples?"

"The one thing I remember was an incident with the ritual of Tinker Day."

Tinker Day became an official holiday for the college in 1895. It is a surprise holiday that is kept secret until students receive a telephone call at 5:00 a.m. or earlier. Students climb Tinker Mountain to a fried chicken lunch at the top. The other part of the day is spent with students performing skits and other fun. Toward the end of the day, students hiked and sometimes slid down Tinker Mountain.

"They had this tradition, which was alien to me coming from a historically black institution, of throwing toilet tissues in the trees. I know if we had done that at Howard University, we would have been put out of school, to say the least. Since I knew the gentlemen who would have to take that toilet tissue out of the trees, I asked the black students not to participate in this ritual because those little old men—and most of them were old; the college didn't hire young black men in 1971—you don't want those men to have to climb trees because of something called fun, which causes that kind of work. I thought there was something very strange about the ritual. The morning that they did that, the black students got up, and not only did they not participate, but they helped to remove the toilet tissue from the trees with the workers. That caused such anger that some of the white students not only told the black students that they didn't belong, but they spat on them."

"Why do you think that the white students acted in such a way?"

"The black students were breaking tradition. And if there's one thing that Hollins College and many like it in the South are known for, it's tradition."

"Did this occurrence get back to the administration? If so, what was the response?"

"Yes, the administration knew because I told them. There was no punishment."

"Do you remember any other race-charged incidents?"

"Yes. I was on a recruiting trip in New York City with one other black student. We received a telephone call in the middle of the night from several black students. They were crying. I asked what was wrong. They answered by saying they 'were done.' There had been a talent show at the college. During the course of the talent show male visitors from the area's male colleges were present and had been actively drinking. In one of the skits were white students wearing afro wigs and dressed like 'natives,' and there was a huge black pot on the stage as well, and in the pot they supposedly were boiling a person. It was the president of the college being boiled. The black students got up as a group and walked out because they were insulted, as I would have been had I been there. As they walked out, the males in the audience called them 'nigger bitches.' The students had come to their rooms so distraught that they called me in

New York and cried on the telephone. Needless to say, we all cried on the telephone that night. When I got back to campus, the black students decided to protest in the courtyard. They informed me beforehand. I said, you must have some organization. Decide what you are protesting and develop issues or else you will not be heard. They developed the issues and asked me to lead them. To add some merit to their issues, I agreed. They gave me the issues and—who's the minister there now?"

"Jan Carruthers, but it would have been Alvord Beardsless."

"That's right. When they had the protest, Reverend Beardsless joined in the circle with the black students and some of the white students as well. I read the demands of the students. It was a peaceful event."

"What were some of the demands?"

"I don't remember specifically, but when I arrived home my telephone rang. It was the president."

"Who was . . . ?"[1]

"I don't know. It was such an emotionally charged time. The president of the college laid me out for participating. I said to him, 'Wait a minute. If you want to know what my role was, you can call Reverend Beardsless. It was a peaceful event that the students had every right to. I had them develop issues and I read them. Now, when students ask me to do that I am going to do it. Don't you ever call this phone line again and tell me what I am supposed to do as an adult.' I really said that. I also said, if there were a question about what I said or what I did, 'you can ask Reverend Beardless. I think that he's a legitimate source. There was nothing I did to encourage any disruption. My role was to control disruption.' "

"Did he know about what had caused the protest?"

"Yes, remember, he was the one in the pot on stage. It was a very interesting time. All of this happened in one year. I was given another contract for the following year, but we—my husband and I—decided to move. Maybe he did check with Reverend Beardsless; I don't know. That was not a concern of mine."

"How would you describe the relationship between the college and the community when you were there?"

"Employer/employee. But for the first time, I believe the college began to see them as more than servants whenever members of the community were guests at the college coming to the different programs at my invitation. One woman from the community said, 'I've been working here for forty years and this is the first time I've been served.' That was a nice thing.

"Hollins College had a policy that faculty and staff members' daughters could go to Hollins College free. If you had a son, they'd give you a thousand dollars toward tuition at another college. You could also use all of the facilities at the college including the library and gym. My husband and I used to go to the gym and play basketball with other faculty members. One of the grandchildren of the workers from the community came to my office and asked if I would check a book out of the library for her because she had to do some research. I informed her that she could go to the library and get it herself. She said, 'No, I can't.' I asked her what did she mean that she couldn't get it. She said, 'We don't have those privileges.'

"Those privileges did not extend to the members of the community. We started questioning that and challenged the use of facilities. Those children deserved the same rights as every other employee's child. Just basic things that were clearly different because of their race and the status that they had. For example, security guards who had no more education than members of the community could use the facilities, but there were no black security guards at that time. It's not difficult to understand. I think lots of times, and I'm not saying anything except it's an observation, that a lot of things were continued practices from days of slavery. People kept doing exactly what they had done until someone raised questions: Have you looked at this? Is this right? It wasn't hard to change those kinds of things. If there is any challenge to having some diversity in every institution, especially those that we call educational institutions, certainly we become blind whenever we see the same thing. It's like driving to work the same route every day. I am often frightened when I have pulled into a parking space and realized my mind has not been on what I was doing since I left my house, because I had blocked it all out. I had seen, but haven't seen all of the traffic lights and I could have killed somebody. It's the same kind of thing with people in that setting. They have killed the spirits of many people. They have left a place and ended up in a destination without understanding the route they took. That's unfortunate. They need to have somebody in the car beside them on their journey to say watch that truck, or that kid, look at what's going on, because they can't see. They have never had anybody there to ask, 'Have you questioned the toilet tissue occurrence?'

"I was on the financial aid committee as an administrator. There was much debate about financial awards. It was just inconceivable to me that people could consider financial aid to people with such assets that some of the students' parents had. It was just a different view. I asked one the faculty members who sat on the committee: 'You don't earn any more money than I do; how can you think that a person who has assets of $250,000 is in need of financial aid?' The tragedy there was that faculty often identified with the class of the parents with money, though they were poor. I said, 'Wait a minute, you earn nine to ten thousand dollars per year: how do you think this way?' I cannot think that way. Even just saying things out loud sometimes made people see a lot of things that they ordinarily wouldn't see, or didn't choose to see. I tell students when you sit and discuss welfare—everybody should work, nobody should be given a hand-out. That's what every student said. Whenever you actually showed them who says this, the people who don't even work, and they will be in that category identifying with people who are so far above them economically. They will never be in that rich category, and they are saying the things that these people who have ironically never worked, who at cocktail parties say we don't want to give anybody any money, and they are getting corporate welfare or their hus-bands are. Here are students who are going to get out of college and at best earn twenty thousand per year if they are lucky. They are going to understand that they can't even earn a living. You identify with the wrong kind of people here because you're not ever going to fit into that 2 percent."

"They are dreaming."

"People tend to dream, and there's nothing wrong with that, but you don't for-get where you are and what's going to happen if you don't get there. If you get there, 99 percent of the others won't, and what about them? Are you going to treat their inability to get to that level, which is impossible because the system won't allow it, or are you going to say they're just lazy, which is an easy cop-out?"

"One of the things that Mrs. Bruce has mentioned to me is that the college changed once it came under the direction of someone who wasn't a Cocke or a Turner. Ironically, during the 1960s the college almost distanced itself from the community completely, other than employer/employee. I found that interesting: that the Civil Rights Movement estranged the college from the community."

"When I arrived that had already happened. I wasn't part of that transition. So the relationship had been a kind of master/slave relationship?"

"Yes. The community members felt that at least there was some sense of accountability. I believe the first major change that happened to that relation-ship was the Depression and later the minimum-wage laws."

"That makes perfect sense."

"Did any of the members of the community ever talk about their ancestry to you?"

"One year is a short time. Not even twelve full months. Because whenever the era ends, you leave. I think about it a lot, but during that one school year, I was a lot younger and had a lot more energy. I developed a lecture series, taught a course, did recruitment, handled every racial incident, and built a program for the short term. I was also head of the human relations counseling for the city of Roanoke. I was a member of the ACLU and all of those other things in the community. It was an interesting time. I don't see how I did all of those things now when I look back."

"Is there anything that I haven't asked you about the college and the com-munity that you would like to discuss?"

"I am sure there is. I just don't know what it is."

"I am still having a hard time with the president of the college calling to chew you out about the students protesting when they were treated so badly. And he was very much part of the problem."

"That's right. He should have understood the outrage. Are you surprised? Not of him, but the situation? Where people are criticized for their reaction rather than the people out here looking at what caused it."

"He was an instigator."

"That's right."

"You should have been calling and chewing him out. He should have been embarrassed for the college."

"I agree, he should have been. I was hired because they had a need, but they were just lucky that it was me."

"They got very lucky."

"The tragedy is that any black person driving in there like I did would not have stayed and tried to serve students, all of the students. I talked about this at a conference in New York. Yes, it could have been anybody, but I believe there are no accidents."

"Are you in touch with any of the students today?"

"Yes; I was closest to Pat Taylor. She died two years ago from cancer. I was in Tyson's Corner, Virginia, last year and I heard someone yell, 'Esther Vassar!' and it was one the students from Hollins when I was there."

"Do you know how I can get in touch with any of the students?"

"Rubye Howard was the student calling me in Tyson's Corner. Patricia McGowan lives in Richmond. I ran into her accidentally two years ago. You can probably look them up in the alumnae directory."[2]

"That would be a good start."

"How many black students are there now?"

"Not thirty. That is as high as it has ever been."

"So those were actually the golden years?"

"I think a lot of things happened in the sixties. It was a cycle."

"Well, they skipped a cycle. Ten years. It has been twenty-five years and they haven't had a renaissance again."

"I can't imagine there will be with regard to the enrollment of African American students. The college is so rooted in tradition."

"They think a black presence only benefits black people. That is an error. Those silly people think that this world is going to accommodate them, and it's not."

"Thank you very much."

Epilogue

From Whence Cometh My Help comes to completion on the dawn of the dedication of the Wyndham Robertson Library at Hollins University. In a speech for the opening convocation, titled "Windows on the World," President Janet Rasmussen quoted the historian Barbara W. Tuchman, "'Books are the carriers of civilization. Without books, history is silent, literature is dumb, science crippled, thought and speculation at a standstill. Without books, the development of civilization would have been impossible.'" It is my hope that *From Whence Cometh My Help* will be a small window on the world of the Hollins Community. Charles Lewis Cocke felt "deeply and passionately about books and reading. He encouraged students to 'adopt books as friends.'"[1] I couldn't agree with him more. I see our new library as a catalyst for communal outreach, particularly in the area of literary action. And no community is more dear to my heart than the Hollins Community. Cocke himself set the standards for its members early on by extending the mission of the college to the community. Records show his deep belief in the education of the Hollins Community; that approach was correct then, and it is still the right thing to do. Charles Lewis Cocke clearly has left Hollins University with a legacy to serve as an instrument of positive change.

I am confident that the university can and will rise to the challenge of its mission that "nurtures civility, integrity, and concern for others, encourages and values diversity and social justice, and affirms the equal worth of women and men."[2] Diversity initiatives are a solid part of the mission of the president and members of the diversity task force. Further, Hollins University has always maintained a history of tradition, excellence, honor, and dignity, but some of that history has been silent. John Callahan, an African-Americanist, writes about Ernest Gaines's fictional community, "the Quarter," one similar to Hollins's: "history tells the story of all the attempts to make known what has happened in the past, but it is not clean, tidy, or pat. Like the human condition it speaks of, history is dirty, messy, chaotic, intuitive, and mysterious. History begins with loose ends, and loose ends it returns, like the human condition that inspires it."[3]

As we enter the twenty-first century, we have come face-to-face with history. Our dignity is somewhere between claiming and embracing it.

Hollins College has always had the courage to change. In 1946 when it adopted a retirement plan, all full-time employees could participate—with the exception of the dining hall and dormitory staff, all of whom were African Americans. In 1976 the plan was amended to include dining hall and dormitory staff. In 1981 the plan was amended once again to change the college's matching contribution for faculty members' retirement accounts to 7.5 percent. For others who participated, the matched amount was 5 percent. And finally, in 1998, change was made where a second option for participation was added. Currently, the university will contribute 2 percent to a retirement account with no contribution made by the employee. If employees elect to contribute 5 percent of their earnings, the university will then match with 8 percent. Like the U.S. Constitution and the Declaration of Independence, the university evolves. However, I still struggle to understand how these changes will affect the lives of Mrs. Emma Bruce, her sister Alice, and most of the other older members of the community, who devoted forty, fifty, and sixty years of service to Hollins University.

As the first African American class president and vice president said in a letter to the alumnae, "Whether or not Hollins is actually changing is something that time will reveal; the process started with our elections, and now we are just trying to keep it moving. With your help in becoming active with the campus, we are sure that we can create an avalanche out of the little snowball that both of us represent." These students understand the importance of their role in the history of the university. They have eased my fears, and I am certain that there will never be another unaccounted for history at Hollins University.

During my research it was important for me to understand the history of other colleges and universities in the area. I wanted to know if this labor practice was an exception or if it was fairly standard. Colleges and universities throughout the South, and even some out of the South, like Princeton University, contained communities of African Americans who served them. For instance, the somewhat newer Randolph-Macon Woman's College and Sweet Briar College were both served by an African American community dominated by women. These communities have endured to this day; also, being relatively younger institutions, their traditions left them more open to progressive change. This is a different experience from men's colleges like Davison, Hampton Sydney, University of Virginia, and Princeton, whose communities all but disappeared over time. Finally, for me, the question is, how were these communities treated by the colleges? Needless to say, there is room for improvement in all cases. I see this as an opportunity for Hollins University to continue its tradition of excellence and become a leader in initiating communal change.

In writing this book, it was my intent to work with an open mind. That does not mean that I did not struggle with my own biases—and there were many. I encountered blank spaces. I never had enough time, and my financial resources were limited. Pure passion for the project pushed me forward. And Mrs. Bruce taught me to be patient with my love. I offer this book to the Hollins Community as a joyful celebration and as a "healing art form" to unsilence its rich and layered history. I am appreciative of the community's work, which is rooted in a long tradition of distinction and excellence. I hope that this book will lift its members to a higher level of dignity, promising the beginning of all that is possible, that a new capacity for communal revision will not just become a part of our missions, but will grow in our hearts. We don't have to go far; if only we'd lift our eyes and see what is already here.

Notes

Chapter 1: In the Beginning

1. William Golding, "The Glass Door," 140. Golding wrote this essay when he was the first writer-in-residence in the creative writing program in 1966.

2. Deedie Kagey, *When Past Is Prologue: A History of Roanoke County*, 130-35.

3. Ibid., 152. "Clairborne" is probably a reference to Clairborne Scott, a free black man who was employed by Cocke.

4. Isaac M. Warren, *Our Colored People*, 11.

5. Notes of Joseph A. Turner, June 28, 1926, Hollins Archives; Kagey, *When Past Is Prologue*, 740.

6. Kagey, *When Past Is Prologue*, 741.

7. Warren, *Our Colored People*, 6–9.

8. Minutes of the Board of Trust of the Valley Union Education Society, March 1864, Hollins Archives.

9. Kagey, *When Past Is Prologue*, 140; Frances J. Niederer, *Hollins College: An Illustrated History*, 9.

10. Jonathan Hughes, *American Economic History*, 257. It seems as though Cocke gave incentive payments to three of his own slaves—Harry, Randall, and Buck—in 1857. Each received five dollars, the equivalent of a week's pay for a manufacturing worker in Botetourt County (see Irwin B. Cohen, *An Economic and Social Survey of Botetourt County*, 97).

11. Catalogue of Hollins Institute, 1876–77, 5. Hollins College did not have a treasurer until 1875, when William H. Pleasants was appointed. Before that, bookkeeping and other financial aspects of the college were handled by the men of the Cocke family.

12. Ibid., 9.

13. It seems that if women workers were known, it was by their tasks rather than by their names. Men were known more by their personalities and in some cases their full names.

Chapter 2: Meet Julius Caesar of Hollins College
1. Newspaper clipping found inserted in the pages of the July 1929 issue of the *Hollins Quarterly* that is in the Hollins Archives.
2. Deed Books of Roanoke County.
3. Ibid.
4. *Hollins Quarterly*, July 1929, 1–2.
5. Ibid.
6. *New York Times*, May 12, 1929.

Chapter 3: I Saw Lee Surrender
1. Box marked "Servants," Hollins Archives.

Chapter 4: Thursday Afternoons
1. Report of the President, Hollins College, July 1934.
2. Frances Niederer writes that in 1939 "a steam laundry to replace the former system of relying on laundresses in the 'old field' " (*Hollins College*, 108). Mrs. Bruce stated, however, that this new laundry system was only used for institutional laundry and did not totally replace the "old field" laundresses.
3. Malinda Morton earned substantial wages as a washerwoman, being bold enough to regularly request payment in kind. However, she only did this after 1871 (Financial Ledgers, 1876, Hollins Archives). Also listed in the ledgers were payments in bacon, bricks, lime, flour, pork, beef, shoes, gloves, fuel, a horse, and a cow.

Chapter 5: Dean of Servants
1. Elizabeth Elliott, "Faithful Friend," *Hollins Alumnae Magazine* 21, no. 3 (spring 1948): 1–2. Elliot was the public secretary of Hollins College.
2. Information from Ruth Bell, Hollins Class of 1958, Rutherfordton, North Carolina. This information is confirmed by Mrs. Bruce and the retirement records of Lewis Hunt.

Chapter 6: The Price of Change
1. Clare White, *Roanoke: 1740–1982*, 86.
2. Ibid., 224–25.
3. Kagey, *When Past Is Prologue*, 280.
4. E. C. Ezeani, "Economic Conditions and Freed Black Slaves in the United States, 1879–1920," 112.
5. Kagey, *When Past Is Prologue*, 290.

6. Ibid., 294.

7. Mary Bishop, "Old Church Is More Than a Memory," *Roanoke Times and World News*, January 18, 1992.

Chapter 8: The Lord Keeps Me

1. Brian Lanke, *I Dream of a World: Portraits of Black Women Who Changed America*, 78.

2. Ibid., 133.

3. Mary Bishop, "Call to Worship." *Roanoke Times and World News*, November 15, 1992.

4. Kagey, *When Past Is Prologue*, 130–35.

5. Minutes of the 1866 Valley Baptist Association of Virginia, Notes of Charles Lewis Cocke, Hollins Archives.

6. Mary Bishop, "Church Gives Thanks for Gift of Hope," July 12, 1993.

7. Mary Bishop, "Old Building, New Landmarks: Baptist Church, New River Home Make Registry," *Roanoke Times and World News*, June 16, 1994.

8. John Reed, *American Vision Magazine*, spring 1997, 83.

Chapter 10: President in a Pot

1. John Arthur Logan was president of Hollins College from 1970 to 1975.

2. I looked up the addresses of the two students and wrote letters to them, but neither responded.

Epilogue

1. Janet Rasmussen, President of Hollins College, "Windows on the World," opening convocation speech, September 2, 1998.

2. From the mission statement of Hollins College.

3. John T. Callahan, "Hearing Is Believing: The Landscape of Voice in Renest Haines's Bloodline," 189.

Bibliography

Andrews, William L. *To Tell a Free Story: The First Century of Afro-American Autobiography, 1760–1865*. Urbana: University of Illinois Press, 1986.

Andrews, William L., ed. *Sisters of the Spirit: Three Black Women's Autobiographies of the Nineteenth Century*. Bloomington: Indiana University Press, 1986.

Ball, Edward. *Slaves in the Family*. New York: Ballantine Books, 1998.

Braxton, Joanne M. *Black Women Writing Autobiography: A Tradition within a Tradition*. Philadelphia: Temple University Press, 1989.

Brooks, Gwendolyn. *Maude Martha*. New York: Harper, 1953.

"Caesar." *The Hollins Quarterly* 4, no. 2 (July 1929): 1–2.

Callahan, John F. "Hearing Is Believing: The Landscape of Voice in Ernest Gaines's Bloodline." *Callaloo* 7, no. 1 (1984): 86–112.

Chestnutt, Charles W. *The Journals of Charles W. Chestnut*. Ed. Richard H. Brodhead. Durham: Duke University Press, 1993.

———. *The Wife of His Youth, and Other Stories of the Color Line*. Boston: Houghton Mifflin, 1899.

Cohen, Irwin B. *An Economic and Social Survey of Botetourt County*. Charlottesville: University Press of Virginia, 1942.

Douglass, Frederick. *The Life and Times of Frederick Douglass*. 1881. Secaucus, N.J.: Citadel Press, 1983.

Du Bois, W. E. B. *The Souls of Black Folk*. New York: Blue Heron Press, 1953. Reprint, New York: Modern Library, 1996.

Early, Gerald, ed. *Lure and Loathing: Essays on Race, Identity, and the Ambivalence of Assimilation*. New York: A. Lane/Penguin Press, 1993.

Ezeani, E. C. "Economic Conditions and Freed Black Slaves in the United States, 1879–1920." In *Review of Black Political Economy*, 104–18. N.p., 1977.

Foster, Francis Smith. *Witnessing Slavery: The Development of Antebellum Slave Narratives*. 2d ed. Madison: University of Wisconsin Press, 1995.

Gaines, Ernest J. *The Autobiography of Miss Jane Pittman*. New York: Dial Press, 1971. Reprint, New York: Bantam Books, 1996.

Gates, Henry Louis, Jr. *The Signifying Monkey: A Theory of Afro-American Literary Criticism*. New York: Oxford University Press, 1988.

Golding, William. "The Glass Door." In *The Hot Gates*. New York: Harcourt, Brace, and World, 1966.

Gutman, Herbert G. *The Black Family in Slavery and Freedom, 1750–1925*. New York: Vintage Books, 1976.

Hughes, Jonathan. *American Economic History*. 3d ed. New York: HarperCollins, 1990.

Hurmence, Belinda. *Before Freedom, When I Just Can Remember: Twenty-Seven Oral Histories of Former South Carolina Slaves*. Winston-Salem, N.C.: J. F. Blair, 1989.

——— *My Folks Don't Want Me to Talk about Slavery: Twenty-One Oral Histories of Former North Carolina Slaves*. Winston-Salem, N.C.: J. F. Blair, 1984.

Hurston, Zora Neale. *Dust Tracks on a Road: An Autobiography*. Ed. Robert Hemenway. Urbana: University of Illinois Press, 1984.

Jackson, Alto L. *Clio, Alabama: A History*. N.p., 1978.

Jacobs, Harriet. *Incidents in the Life of a Slave Girl*. 1861. New York: Oxford University Press, 1988.

Kagey, Deedie. *When Past Is Prologue: A History of Roanoke County*. Roanoke: Roanoke Sesquicentennial Commission, 1988.

Kornweibi, Theodore J. "An Economic Profile of Black Life in the Twenties." *Journal of Black Studies* 6 (1976): 307–20.

Lanke, Brian, photographs and interviews; Barbara Summers, ed. *I Dream a World: Portraits of Black Women Who Changed America*. New York: Stewart, Tabori, and Chang, 1989.

Lewis, Helen, and Suzanna O'Donnell. *Remembering Our Past, Building Our Future: The Ivanhoe History Project*. Ivanhoe, Va.: Ivanhoe Civic League, 1990.

Madden, T. O., Jr., with Ann L. Miller. *We Were Always Free: The Maddens of Culpeper County, Virginia: A 200-Year Family History*. New York: Norton, 1992.

McDowell, Deborah E., and Arnold Rampersad, eds. *Slavery and the Literary Imagination*. Baltimore: John Hopkins University Press, 1989.

McFeely, William S. *Frederick Douglass*. New York: Norton, 1991.

Morrison, Toni. *Beloved*. New York: Alfred A. Knopf, 1987.

Niederer, Frances J. *Hollins College: An Illustrated History*. Charlottesville: University Press of Virginia, 1973.

Painter, Nell Irvin. *Sojourner Truth: A Life, A Symbol*. New York: Norton, 1996.

Pleasants, Mary M. *Which One? and Other Ante Bellum Days*. Boston: James H. Earle, 1910.

Smith, Valerie. *Self-Discovery and Authority in Afro-American Narrative*. Cambridge: Harvard University Press, 1987.

Sterling, Dorothy, ed. *We Are Your Sisters: Black Women in the Nineteenth Century*. New York: Norton, 1984.

Stevens, George Raymond. *An Economic and Social Survey of Roanoke County*. Charlottesville: University Press of Virginia 1930.

Walker, Alice. *The Color Purple*. New York: Harcourt Brace Jovanovich, 1982.

Walker, Margaret. *Jubilee*. Boston: Houghton Mifflin, 1966.

Warren, Isaac M. *Our Colored People*. Roanoke: Federal Writer's Project, 1941.

Washington, Booker T. *Up from Slavery: An Autobiography*. 1901. New York: Dover Publications, 1995.

Washington, Mary Helen, ed. *Black-Eyed Susans: Classic Stories by and about Black Women*. New York: Anchor Press, 1975.

White, Clare. *Roanoke, 1740–1982*. Roanoke: Roanoke Valley Historical Society, 1982.

White, Deborah Gray. *Ar'n't I a Woman? Female Slaves in the Plantation South*. New York: Norton, 1983.

Wilson, Harriet E. *Our Nig, or Sketches from the Life of a Free Black, in a Two-Story White House, North, Showing That Slavery's Shadows Fall Even There*. 1859. New York: Vintage Books, 1983.

Index